ONE MAN'S CRUSADE FOR AN HONEST TARIFF

THE STORY OF HERBERT E. MILES, FATHER OF THE TARIFF COMMISSION

By

N. I. STONE

Formerly Chief Economist
U. S. Tariff Board

THE LAWRENCE COLLEGE PRESS
APPLETON, WIS.

TABLE OF CONTENTS

Page

INTRODUCTORY STATEMENT _____ 2

Chapter

  I THE STRUGGLE FOR A TARIFF COMMISSION 3

  II THE FIGHT AGAINST SPECIAL INTERESTS ON GOVERNMENT BODIES _____ 68

  III THE THIRTEEN-YEAR WAR ON THE SUGAR TARIFF _____ 79

      1. A CHALLENGING REDEFINITION OF TARIFF PROTECTION _____ 79

      2. FRONTAL ATTACK ON THE SUGAR TARIFF ____ 82

  IV CRIME, PINEAPPLES AND THE TARIFF COMMISSION _____ 89

  V THE FORDNEY–McCUMBER TARIFF _____ 93

  VI THE HAWLEY–SMOOT TARIFF _____ 99

  VII MILES ON TRUSTS _____ 110

  VIII CONCLUSION _____ 112

HERBERT EDWIN MILES, 1860–1939

Herbert Edwin Miles came to Lawrence College in the fall of 1877 to attend first the preparatory school and later the College. He graduated from the latter in 1882, valedictorian of his class and winner of the Lewis Prize, the award which has been given at Lawrence each year now for almost a century to the scholar of most excellent record.

Mr. Miles' active business career was carried on first in Waupaca, Wisconsin, and later in Racine. But he was always a man of ranging interests and was almost constantly involved in a great variety of extra-professional activity, much of it at a national level. He was one of the founders of the National Chamber of Commerce and an officer of the National Association of Manufacturers. He was for many years Chairman of the Fair Tariff League. And he played a leading role in the development of vocational educational institutions in Wisconsin and more widely.

A lover of art, an active mind, and an energetic spirit, he had his eye always, in his own phrase, on "a better tomorrow" and worked constantly as best he could in many enterprises throughout his life for the moral betterment of mankind. Lawrence College is proud to sponsor this publication in honor of a distinguished alumnus.

NATHAN M. PUSEY, *President*
Lawrence College

Appleton, Wisconsin
April 12, 1952

HERBERT E. MILES,
Chairman Executive Committee, Chamber of Commerce of the United States

I. THE STRUGGLE FOR A TARIFF COMMISSION

THIS IS the story of an American pioneer. A manufacturer, a Republican, and an avowed protectionist, his moral indignation was aroused by his discovery of "graft in the tariff." From that moment he went about championing the cause of tariff reform with single-minded devotion. Although it lacked broad popular appeal at first, his persistence, his courageous leadership triumphed in the end and he was able to bring it to a successful culmination, sweeping aside entrenched interests and formidable opposition by leaders in Congress.

Herbert Edwin Miles was born at Waupaca, Wisconsin, Nov. 21, 1860 and died in Madison in his native state on August 6, 1939 at the age of 79. He was educated at Lawrence College and at Harvard. As a young man he went into business and became president of the Racine Wagon and Carriage Company. The business prospered, was merged with the Sattley Company, manufacturing agricultural implements, and Mr. Miles became president of the Racine-Sattley Company of Racine, Wisconsin.

With his inquiring bent of mind, and an education greatly superior to that of the average business man of his time, it was natural that his intellectual interests should carry him beyond the confines of his own business. In spite of his exacting duties as executive of a fair-sized manufacturing business, which had to meet open competition, he became interested in the broader aspects of national economic problems as they affected business. His was the spirit of the early American pioneer and he was not afraid to push beyond existing frontiers and tread new ground.

He was an active member of the National Association of Manufacturers in the early years of this century when the association was presided over by James W. Van Cleave who attracted nation-wide attention by his aggressive leadership of the Association. Mr. Miles was named Chairman of its Tariff Committee.

A sincere believer in the beneficent effects of protection he approached his new task as Chairman of the Tariff Committee with the sole aim of doing his best to help spread the benefits of the protective tariff to all American industries and to all who earned their living in industry—from the man who risked his capital in industrial enterprise to his workmen and their dependents.

His faith in protection was not the result of profound study. It came to him, like religion, from the environment and the general mental climate of an industrial community whose industries sprang up and grew apace under the protective tariff system. Never having lived under any other system, the industrial community took tariff protection for granted, as natural as the natural resources from which it drew its raw materials and as American as the Constitution and the Federal and State Governments.

As a manufacturer of agricultural implements and wagons, Miles was a consumer of steel, the product of the newly organized U. S. Steel Corporation. In the course of his business experience as a buyer of steel, Mr. Miles discovered that the domestic price of steel came to be higher than the export price by approximately the amount of the tariff. As a result, he was no longer able to compete with European manufacturers of agricultural implements in their markets where they could buy American steel cheaper than he could at home.

This discovery caused him to look more closely into the tariff. The study confirmed his practical experience and he reluctantly came to the conclusion that the tariff then in force erred or sinned in two respects: first, that the products of the "trusts", (by which he meant big corporations of the type of U. S. Steel), enjoying a commanding position in the market, were overprotected, i.e. received protection far in excess of what could be reasonably justified; and second, that they were unduly favored at the expense of the small companies which had to buy their materials from the big concerns. As his intellectual horizon broadened out to take in the national scene, he saw that what he had first regarded as a problem of his own individual business was of national significance. The problem, originating in national legislation, obviously called for remedial legislation on a national scale.

The turn of the century also marked a turn in our tariff policy. McKinley first came into national prominence as a Congressman, through the enactment of the McKinley Tariff Act in 1891. The McKinley tariff raised our import duties to what was then the highest point in American history. It was swept off the statute books in Grover Cleveland's administration by the enactment of the Democratic Wilson Act of 1894 which, in turn, remained in force only three years, to give way to the Dingley Act of 1897 in the McKinley Administration.

The progress made by American industry in the last two decades of the Nineteenth Century was phenomenal. It found its culmination in the organization of gigantic corporations which became commonly known as "trusts" after Standard Oil was organized in the form of a legal trust. It was the period marked by the advent of the first industrial combine in the billion dollar class, when J. P. Morgan brought about the billion-and-a-half dollar consolidation of the steel industry in the U. S. Steel Corporation.

Most of these large corporations, led by Standard Oil and U. S. Steel, became interested in export trade as an outlet for the surplus of their output over the requirements of the domestic markets. They soon discovered that one of the effects of the McKinley tariff of

[5]

1891 was the adoption of protective tariffs by several European countries with Germany and France in the lead. These tariffs had a new feature—a double set of duties, the lower set being extended to imports from countries with which they had either reciprocity or most favored nation treaties, and the higher being applicable to all other countries. The United States fell in the latter category.

A demand arose among manufacturers interested in export trade, for reciprocity arrangements with European countries. It was in response to these demands that the Dingley Tariff of 1897, with duties far in excess of the McKinley rates, provided for reciprocal reductions of duty. This provision took a twofold form:

Section 4 of the Dingley Act authorized the President to negotiate reciprocity treaties under which he could grant reductions of duty not to exceed 20%, on various products for a period not exceeding five years in return for reciprocal reductions on American products. These treaties were subject to ratification by the U. S. Senate. The other provision, contained in Section 3, authorized the President to make moderate reductions of duty on a few articles, mostly wines, paintings and statuary, in return for reciprocal concessions, wholly at his discretion without the need of Senate approval.

President McKinley put his heart into the new dispensation and appointed John A. Kasson as Commissioner to negotiate the treaties. Several treaties were negotiated but not one was approved by the Senate. President McKinley was greatly upset by this development. He who had earned the title of High Priest of Protection had become convinced that new conditions called for new measures. The last speech he delivered at the Buffalo Exposition on September 5, 1901, only a day before he was assassinated, was devoted to a plea for a change in our tariff policy. His words: "the period of exclusiveness is past. . . . Reciprocity is the natural outgrowth of our wonderful industrial development", rang out as a dramatic call to the country and marked the beginning of the movement for tariff reduction through reciprocity.

President Theodore Roosevelt was in sympathy with the views of his predecessor but, preoccupied with his fight for reforms in other fields, took no initiative in the struggle for tariff reform.

While the movement for tariff reciprocity was initiated by industry, a similar movement was slowly taking shape among the agricultural interests. At the turn of the century, more than 65% of our exports consisted of agricultural products and the farmer was far more dependent upon foreign trade than was the manufacturer. Numerous farmers' organizations, including the Grange, were wrought up over the tariff. The farmer felt that the price of wheat, cotton and other agricultural products was fixed in Europe so that he got no benefit from the tariff, while he was made to pay excessive prices on everything he bought because of the tariff on manufactured goods.

The new tariff adopted by Germany in the Christmas week of 1902, did not take effect until 1906. It greatly raised existing rates on agricultural products and imported meats and tightened inspection rules on live and slaughtered animals, thus threatening to choke off our hitherto growing and lucrative exports to Germany. The newly adopted tariff rates and regulations were part of the so-called general (i.e. maximum) tariff. They were open to reduction and modification through negotiations for reciprocal concessions during the three year interval between the adoption of the general tariff and the time the conventional (i.e. minimum) tariff was to go into effect.

This situation spurred Alvin H. Sanders, Chicago publisher of the Breeders' Gazette, to start a movement which culminated in the formation of the American Reciprocal Tariff League of which Sanders became President. It embraced a large number of farmers' organizations and had additional financial backing from the Chicago meatpackers.

Sanders favored reductions of American tariff rates as the price to be paid for reductions of German tariff rates on American meats and food animals. Miles wanted reductions of American tariff rates as an act of justice to the American consumer and the small manufacturer who suffered at the hands of the "trusts".

Besides becoming Chairman of the Tariff Committee of the National Association of Manufacturers, Miles was also President of the National Association of Agricultural Implement and Vehicle Manufacturers. As an orthodox, sincere and honest protectionist, Miles took at its face value the current assertion that the object of the tariff was to protect the high standard of American labor from "the pauper labor" in foreign countries and reasoned out the formula that the tariff should equal the difference between American labor costs and those of competing foreign countries. As we shall see later, he succeeded in winning over President Roosevelt and William Howard Taft to this formula and the latter championed it in his successful campaign for the Presidency.

The more Miles studied the intricacies of the tariff, the more he was driven to the conclusion that it favored big business at the expense of the small manufacturer. He was disgusted with the sloppy methods of the Congressional committees which accepted extravagant, unsupported statements by interested parties as conclusive evidence for the rates of duty they demanded. He was indignant when the conviction slowly dawned upon him that important basic rates in the tariff were written by the lobbyists of big business and accepted without question by the House Ways and Means Committee and the Senate Finance Committee.

As Chief of the Division of Foreign Tariffs in the Department of Commerce I was at that time engaged in a detailed study of the European methods of tariff making. In two "North American Review" articles I reviewed the tariff relations between the United States and Germany which were then reaching a breaking point. I described the elaborate method of tariff making in Germany where it had taken five years of study and preparation to enact the new tariff and two additional years to negotiate reciprocity treaties (or conventions, as the Germans called them) with foreign countries, after which another year was allowed to elapse to enable German business to adjust itself to the new tariff before it was to take effect and remain in force under the treaties for a period of not less than twelve years.

The articles caught the attention of both Sanders and Miles and each approached me for more information. In time the requests for information developed into requests for advice and these separate consultations eventually developed into a council of three.

Sanders was impressed by the frustration of President McKinley's efforts to negotiate reciprocity treaties under the Dingley Act of 1897. Miles was determined to put his best efforts into a movement to end the old method of Congressional tariff making which allowed interested parties to fix basic tariff rates behind the scenes and then to have them enacted into law by the time-honored method of logrolling on the floor of each house of Congress.

All of this resulted in the decision to launch a movement with a threefold goal: 1) The establishment by an act of Congress of a permanent Tariff Commission of impartial experts; the Commission to be engaged in a continuous study of costs of production at home and in competing foreign countries of all products covered by the tariff. 2) Enactment of tariff rates by Congress on the basis of reports of the Tariff Commission as to comparative costs of various products, the tariff rates to be equal to the difference in costs of production of such products at home and in competing foreign countries. 3) Empowering the President to negotiate reciprocity agreements within limits set by the Congress in the Tariff Act without the necessity of ratification by a two-thirds majority vote in the Senate.

With the objectives thus clearly formulated Miles and Sanders rolled up their sleeves and each launched a strong movement in his own field: Sanders, through his American Reciprocal Tariff League among the farmers, particularly among the stock-breeders in the West, while Miles got busy in the industrial field through the National Association of Agricultural Implement and Vehicle Manufacturers and National Association of Manufacturers.

In the popular conception of the tariff, industry is regarded as the chief if not the sole beneficiary of protection and the prime mover of all tariff legislation. The appeal for tariff reduction is therefore directed to the consumer. Unfortunately the consuming public is not organized and carries little weight in the minds of Congressional leaders. In probing the tariff, however, Miles, as already stated, was shocked to discover that far from an even-handed protection being extended to all industry, there was a distinct pattern of excessive protection to industries controlled by large powerful corporations, the "trusts", at the expense of the small manufacturer who uses the product of the big corporation as his raw material. He, therefore, felt he could make his appeal for downward revision of the tariff to the great body of small manufacturers who numerically constitute the overwhelming majority of industrial enterprises.

The Report of the Special Tariff Committee of the National Association of Agricultural Implement and Vehicle Manufacturers, constituting the first shot fired by Miles in his campaign, is an interesting historical document because it is the first instance, to my knowledge, of an incipient revolt of an organized industry against the excesses of the protective tariff, presumably enacted for its benefit. Because of this circumstance and of the interesting facts it reveals it deserves to be quoted in extenso.

Addressing the Executive Committee of the Association in the fall of 1906, Miles said:

On April 10, 1906, by vote of your Committee, it was decided that a Committee

"be authorized and directed to investigate the entire question of the *Tariff and Reciprocity* in their bearing upon the industries represented in this Association; such Committee to report the results of its work to the Executive Committee."

As such Committee we submit this—our report. That you may know our general attitude, we state that *each of us is a thorough Protectionist,* as that *term is reasonably defined. We believe implicitly in protection to American industries and to American labor* in its enjoyment of a high wage scale, and in President Roosevelt's measure of Protection as "the difference between the scale of wages here and the scale of wages abroad"—this difference to be measured not by the daily rate of wages, but by the wage cost per unit of production. This belief with us is unqualified and militant. We hold it, as we believe, in common with practically our entire membership and with 90% of the American people. It is not, therefore, with us a question of the theory of Protection. It is wholly of the fair and reasonable application of that theory. A good theory misapplied is no better than a bad theory logically applied. We confine ourselves, therefore, to a question of application or, in other words, of Existing Schedules.

Our members are interested chiefly in hides, which are used by our carriage builders only; in steel, used by us all; and in lumber, used by us all, but in particular measure by our farm wagon builders.

LEATHER

We find no need nor justice in the present tariff on leather and hides. The President's definition permits of none. It is not a matter of wage adjustment, as there is little labor in the making of the fresh hide, as the wage cost of converting into sole leather is estimated at 6% or less of the sales price. For twenty-five years prior to 1897, there was no such tariff. At this time, there is no tariff except upon cattle hides weighing more than twenty-five pounds each, consequently a great many cattle hides are trimmed down to a less weight than twenty-five pounds, and imported free. Almost all heavier hides imported are imported in bond and exported in finished products, so that the Government derives almost no revenue from this tariff. It is a matter of common belief, if not of knowledge, that the so-called Beef Trust and the Leather Trust, owned by the Beef Trust, profit greatly from this tariff to the needless expense of the consumer.

Some 300,000,000 pairs of shoes are consumed in the United States annually, and the extra cost of the same, consequent upon the tariff, has been estimated by experts at $30,000,000 per year. The loss to the carriage industry has not been figured, but is in proportion. The prices of carriage leathers have advanced from 20% to 40% under this tariff.

The present hide schedules have few or no supporters among the stock growers or leather makers so far as we can learn, except some of the large raisers in the far West.

The packers, themselves, have declared very positively that they are entirely willing, if not desirous, for the removal of the tariff as a factor in general Revision and Reciprocity; the tanners likewise; while those who make up the leather into finished products are unanimously and aggressively desirous of its removal. The cost of leather has come to be so high to the carriage builder, that he is tempted to use cheaper and cheaper grades to the detriment of the wearing quality and service of the vehicle in respect to its leather. *The leather bill of the carriage maker is greater than his bills for any other two materials. Greater, for instance, than the charge for the steel and the lumber combined.* It is a very great item with him, and we can but believe that an active declaration and effort toward the removal of this tariff would be for the great benefit of our carriage making members and the consumers of their product.

As stated, we have found no one dealing in either hides or leather, who expresses other than an affirmative opinion on this subject.

STEEL

Every member is a large user of steel, our implement makers depending upon it as practically their sole material. Accepting again of President Roosevelt's measure of the degree of Protection needed, being such an amount as perfectly protects the American manufacturer against his foreign rival and the American laborer in his present wage, we find as follows:

ORE: Our ore beds have now in great measure come under monopolistic control. Ore within our borders is now a scarce commodity. There is, however, practically an unlimited supply on this continent, and with free ore under a reciprocal or other agreement with Canada and other countries, ore would again be as easily obtainable as in years back when the price of steel to our members was little more than half the present price.

The labor cost of mining ore is often cheaper per ton in this country than anywhere else. The cost is in places, and for great quantities, as low as five cents per ton for loading upon the cars out of the native beds. Train loads of 35 to 40 cars, each of 50 tons capacity, have been loaded with steam shovels in two hours. "A forty ton car of coal can be unloaded and partially trimmed in the ship in thirty-six seconds. . . ."

Speaking broadly, we find no reason to question the statement that the cost of ore in this country and of transportation to the furnace is as low as anywhere else in the world, and in Alabama lower than anywhere else in the world. Every one knows that transportation in America is cheaper than elsewhere.

We, therefore, find no substantial reason or justice in a protective tariff on these raw materials, much less in what is now practically a *prohibitive* tariff.

PIG IRON. The wage cost at the furnace of converting raw material into a ton of molten pig averages throughout this country 90 cents per ton produced. It is as low at one furnace as 70 cents. The tariff is $4.00. The cost at the furnace of converting the raw materials into a ton of pig iron, including incidentals, maintenance and repairs, averages throughout the United States about $1.65 per ton of pig produced. The present unreasonable tariff is, therefore, over three times the *wage cost* at the furnace, and over twice total cost of conversion at the furnace, exclusive of raw materials, including allowance for incidentals, maintenance and repairs. It exceeds the average total labor cost of mining, transporting and melting. We pronounce this wholly unreasonable and unjust.

STEEL BARS: We have found no expert who places the cost of steel bars made by the continuous process at more than 90 cents per hundred pounds, or $18.00 per ton. You will remember we used to buy it for $16.00 per ton at mill a few years ago, believing then that there was at least no loss to the producers at this price. The *Iron Age,* Feb. 1st last, says of one great producer:

"The cost of production has been cut down at least $2.00 per ton since 1901."

A remarkable statement, in view of the great increase in the general rate of wages, cost of living, etc.

Some of our evidence is to the effect that steel can be produced for not to exceed $16.00 per ton, or slightly more than one-half of the present market price. Steel is made cheaper in Alabama than anywhere else on earth, and about as cheaply elsewhere in the United States as abroad. This statement was recently confirmed by one of the representative steel men of the country before Congressional Committee. Yet the tariff is $10.00 a ton and in excess of the total wage cost. We know of independent mills who make 80% profit on their capital per annum at the present prices.

We cannot question the mass of evidence before us to the effect that steel has for years been sold to foreign users at 25% to 30% below the market price to American purchasers, and as one concern shipped abroad over 950,000 tons last year, we must believe that there is a satisfactory profit to the producer at the foreign price. We have evidence also that steel products, including bolts, saws, etc., are ofttimes sold abroad in large quantities at 30% to 40% below the prices charged us.

In this respect our present Schedules are not protective, but grossly discriminative. They make the wall so high that the home consumer cannot reach over it, compelling him to pay very high prices to a few producers, while he sees those same producers go through the wall out to the foreigner, happy in

[14]

making to that foreigner prices 20% to 30% less on great quantities of merchandise than charged the home consumer. And our Congressional Representatives refuse point blank to meet the issue.

It is unnecessary for us to state the situation as regards the mutual understandings of the steel makers and the great measure of our helplessness in the way of securing prices based in any degree upon completion or cost of production. . . .

The Effect of the present prices on steel is seen in our diminished profits. Costs have greatly advanced, while competition has prevented a proportional increase in sales price. Also a loss of foreign trade is threatened. One of our largest implement exporters declares he sees the speedy loss of all his foreign business, due principally to the *increased* cost in his material. A far greater part of the 950,000 tons of steel exported by one producer at low prices last year should have gone abroad in plows, and other finished shapes, to the various countries, rather than direct from the rolls in relatively crude form.

LUMBER

The lumber situation is acute. It is a matter of common belief, if not of knowledge, that there are lumber trusts and associations, which are mainly responsible for the exceeding advance in lumber in the past few years, the price having gone up 100% in a short period. Further advances are to be expected immediately. We are creditably informed that the members of a lumber association or pool, issued six price lists in twelve months, each, of course, an advance. We seem entirely helpless under the present conditions and obliged to pay whatever price is quoted us. We find some reason to believe that the understanding among the producers is so complete that the number of firms who will quote any one buyer is restricted by agreement. Add to this situation the rapid destruction of our forests, and the fact that in all probability arrangements could be made by reciprocal agreements to draw very largely upon the Canadian and other foreign reserves. . . .

OTHER COMMODITIES

Other commodities are in principal measure in much the same situation as those above noted.

No reasonable definition of Protection justifies the *Coal Schedule*. Coal is a prime necessity. Trusts control it, and at times fight with one another over it. Their chief weapon in this warfare is famine and the fear of famine. We helplessly and submissively pay any price asked for it, often hoard it, and at times, in pinching alarm, would steal it as the railroads do. Sane and adequate Revision will again make it and its consumption subject to the simple and old-time laws of trade. If, at any time, domestic interests will not supply it fairly, it will come as ship's ballast, or over foreign rails, and we will live in reason and comfort by grace of foreign supply. . . .

The scientifically constructed tables of Dun and Bradstreet declare that prices of commodities as a whole have advanced since the enactment of the present tariff from 42% to 46%. The prices of our own products, which are made and sold by the old-time free and competitive methods, have advanced less than a third of this per cent. Some of our members have added so little of the increased cost to their prices that they are in serious danger from decreased margins. Others have so increased their prices that any reduction in cost will flow directly to the consumer either in immediate price reduction or partly in price reduction, and partly in better quality.

PUBLIC SENTIMENT

We find a tremendous public sentiment favoring strenuous and concerted action along the lines here indicated. Presidents McKinley and Roosevelt long since asked for it. The National Association of Manufacturers has ordered a poll of its membership with a view of ascertaining its interests. Your Committee has interviewed very many of the leading members of our Association, and has failed to find one but is for taking up this subject, and most of them are very positive in this.

At a recent Convention of American Manufacturers, representing the most diverse interests, nothing was more vigorously applauded than the statement that 80% of the American people are for Revision, with the two extremes representing 10% "Stand Pat," and 10% Free Trade; this 20% being in opposition to the interests of the entire country.

RECIPROCITY

In the foregoing, we have shown that there is ample reason for public relief in the way of tariff adjustment. That fact is itself evidence that there is very ample margin for adjustment of Schedules with foreign nations in the interest of mutual and increased trade. Our membership is extremely interested in this subject; in prime measure with Canada, whose wheat field in the Northwest is 900 miles long, and from 300 to 600 miles wide, and whose people want our goods. . . .

Likewise, though in lesser measure, our interests can be furthered in other foreign countries. Germany, for instance, imports $250,000,000 worth of foodstuffs annually; only one-fifth of this comes from us. She is insisting upon fairer trade with us, and is prepared to double or treble her orders for the products of our farms.

Much is said of the large amount of our manufactured goods exported. Not enough is made of the fact that these exports consist principally of materials like copper, petroleum and steel bars—products which are advanced little beyond the crude state.

America is still a big stevedore bearing down to the ships of the sea crude and semi-crude materials. Reciprocity and Revision with their present large trading margins will further increase the exportation of these materials and add thereto countless millions' worth of those highly finished products which alone will disclose to the world the degree of our efficiency as a manufacturing people. . . .

Last year's crop in this country was raised, as estimated by our Agricultural Department, at a saving of $685,000,000 over the cost of raising an equal crop fifty years ago. Every machine used in raising last year's crop was made by our members. We made every wagon that helped to bear that crop to market. It was the ability of our predecessors, ourselves and our employes that effected this saving upon a single crop—a saving almost equal to the National debt. The merit of our goods is recognized alike at home and abroad. Why are we unsuccessful in foreign trade?

[17]

We hear that the exportation of agricultural implements is increasing. It may be. Twice five cents is a dime. We do not want a mere increase. We want to buy our materials as we sell our products, on a competitive basis, fair profits, fair price, and a fair chance under Reciprocity, not merely to sample a few countries, with a wholly insignificant total, but to supply foreign users in great measure. We only, among the great agricultural nations of the world, are great as manufacturers. Our combined manufacturing and agricultural experience should make us far and away the greatest provider of agricultural implements in other countries. As it is, members of this Committee, while tenaciously struggling to retain foreign trade, are expecting to lose it, and find it more and more difficult to retain, because alike of the excessive cost of their materials and of hostile tariff legislation in foreign countries. Notwithstanding an occasional assertion to the contrary from those evidently unfamiliar with the situation, our goods are made upon a closely competitive basis and a small margin of profit, and are sold at the same price at home and abroad. No further concessions are possible for the holding of foreign trade. Our carriage and wagon builders have wholly given up efforts to sell in Canada and some other countries; our plow members are losing out. Our membership may properly require of our Association any reasonable efforts possible for the betterment of this situation. Before this, by fairer tariffs and fairer costs of materials, we should have strengthened our positions abroad as against the lessened home demand we must expect with the first short crop or financial pinch. . . .

TIME FOR ACTION

It is always said that this question cannot be considered without commercial upheaval and distress, and will not be considered except in time of panic or crop failure. This, however, was said of the Railroad Rate and other questions. We believe the time to consider such questions is when the Nation financially is as now in good health and high spirits.

It is known to us that some gentlemen, prominently identified with the great steel companies and iron mines, are convinced that tariff rates on steel should be immediately revised. They know some of the rates are too high and merely make hostile criticism just. They further urge that the proper time to change the rates is now, when business is good and can be easily adjusted to new rates.

The protected interests make it strictly a matter of business to maintain high rates. They are always earnestly watchful and active. We must not fear beginning too soon. Statements known to all our members to be untrue and misleading are made in high places to influence public sentiment. Our membership are practically unanimous in favoring earnest, high-minded, conservative procedure in behalf of Revision and Reciprocity, for the good alike of ourselves, our 150,000 employes, the 8,000,000 farmers whose implements and vehicles we make, and the general public.

BURDEN OF PROOF

The money in the National Treasury belongs to the Nation. The money in the pockets of the consumers belongs to the consumers. The protected interests ask to take from the pockets of the consumers more money under the Protective System and special Congressional action than they could take, except for such action. The *Burden of Proof* is therefore wholly upon these protected interests. The entire Nation substantially is committed to Protection, as are almost all the other nations of the earth. It is unnecessary for over-protected interests to prate unceasingly upon the desirability of Protection. It is for them to talk of the amount of Protection which a great and marvelously progressive country may rightly be asked to give them. In other words, it is for them to bring forward their figures and justify Schedules.

TARIFF COMMISSION

In this connection we most earnestly urge that our Association recommend to Congress and the President the institution of a *Tariff Commission* of a semi-judicial character with, for instance, power to summon witnesses; this Commission to study thoroughly and scientifically the Tariff question and Reciprocity as a whole, and also each Schedule separately, and embody its findings from time to time in the form of recommendations to Congress and the Executive. Only by some such method is it likely that the element of insincerity will be eliminated. When this is done, as it surely will be in time, the whole subject will be found to be one of Schedules and not of theory; and scientific tables of cost in this country and abroad will make the matter relatively simple and take from the discussion the present element of insincerity and "bluff."

We also recommend a Dual Tariff of *Maximum and Minimum Schedules,* with power vested in the Executive to make treaties of Reciprocity within the limits of this tariff. . . .

CONCLUSION

In conclusion, we re-affirm our implicit belief in the fundamental principles of Protection, and their application to the conservation of American manufacturing interests, including the maintenance of a high wage scale as necessary alike for the employer and the wage earner, and for a proper standard of citizenship.

Equally strong and determined is our disbelief in tariff schedules which now convert Protection into Prohibition, and foster monopoly. Protection largely has made us what we are. It has proven itself out. Rather than denounce, let us rejoice that the time for change has come, when continuance of present schedules would be rank robbery, when material reductions must be made, and the advantages of lessened cost come as a reward for past wisdom and expenditure.

When Revision comes, as all expect it speedily will, let it not be Revision only, but adequate Revision. After the last tariff was enacted, very important steel producers went to Washington and complained that the present schedules were too high. Let the buyers' side be heard next time. This with determination, but without animosity. The protected interests are large-minded and, we believe, disposed to fair dealing. They are expecting Revision soon and ready, as always, to bargain for it.

Congress has at times been very one-sided, but usually only when the interests of the other side have been conspicuously unrepresented. The Revision sentiment in Congress now is strong. Our interests and our information should be made known to the public, and to those who, in principal measure, will determine the next schedules.

Having fired the first broadside through the Association of Implement and Vehicle Manufacturers in the fall of 1906, Miles was ready with his second round in the form of the report of his Tariff Committee of the National Association of Manufacturers, which met in May 1907. This report throwing, as it does, a revealing light on the attitude toward the tariff of a representative cross-section of American industry of that period, also deserves extensive reproduction.

REPORT

New York, May 22, 1907.

Mr. President and Members of the Association:

At the last annual meeting this Association, believing that the question of Tariff Revision and Reciprocity is becoming a paramount issue, and that it is of the greatest importance in that event that this question be adjusted with such care as to cause the least disturbance of the prosperous condition of business, instructed its Tariff Committee to secure the views of all the members, and to harmonize the interests of all, and be in position correctly and definitely to express the wishes of all. . . .

It has been said that each industry can best care for its own schedules. Certainly, each industry best knows its own costs and necessities, and there is a limit beyond which a Joint Committee, as it were, should not go. It is, however, greatly to be desired that there be some committee like that of this Association, which, while not going minutely into each particular interest, by getting data from all, is an efficient factor in harmonizing those interests, that injury be not done to many in the advancement of any one.

Out of 1,368 members who have expressed themselves on the desirability of the continuance of the investigation and work of the Tariff Committee, 1,320 say yes and 48 say no. Taken by industries, 76 industries say yes, 1 says no, the latter casting only two votes.

We are all Protectionists—there are a very few brilliant exceptions, but so few that we may repeat the statement, "We are Protectionists."

Those great forefathers who made the Declaration of Independence and framed the Constitution of the United States, also, with equal wisdom, as one of the first acts of the new Government, adopted and made effective the principle of Protective duties. Our national development—physical and intellectual—is a proud evidence of the wisdom and the success of that policy.

It has a few critics who object, saying that we cannot attribute our entire success to protection, as sometimes it seems to them that we do. We reply: "On the other hand there is no accounting for our present position of unexampled success and prosperity without giving great credit to the effect of the protective policy."

In a republic like ours, where every man votes and is the equal of every other man before the law and as a voting unit, it is essential to the prosperity—and possibly to the very existence—of the republic, that wages be high; and the standard of living, of comfort and of education be correspondingly higher than in the great competing countries of Europe. We may go farther yet and say, that apart from the consideration of necessity, it is the joy and pride of all our citizenship that we can, and do, by protection and high wages, make homes happier and lives better to the great mass of people than elsewhere obtains.

Happy would we be if we need never go beyond this consideration of the general principle, its beneficence, and all that, but there is another phase of the subject where disagreement and discontent not only begin, but are fast coming to dominate.

We must look clearly and fairly at the particular cause of discontent and hurt. In the language of Judge Gary, of the U. S. Steel Corporation: "Those who occupy positions of responsibility and influence must foster dispositions to improve their methods and get into a condition where they will be above reproach and attack. If the men who are complaining of movements calculated to bring exposure and to rectify wrongs will, themselves, become investigators and reformers, they need fear no attacks from others."

[22]

First, as to the facts. Protection, as the word implies, requires that the Tariff Schedules be such as PROTECT our manufacturers against undue pressure from foreign competition, and maintain our high wage scale and standard of living. The MINIMUM measure of protection is, therefore, as President Roosevelt said, "The difference in the cost of production in this country and abroad." These Protective Schedules, thus figured, must carry with them a very ample margin for safety. It must make full allowance for the possibility of hard times abroad and good times here; for dumping, and all other contingencies. This done, it is truly protective; and it is only so, as it covers these features and nothing more. Insofar as Tariff Schedules are higher than this, they are not protective, but are either unjust and discriminatory, or higher for reasons of revenue only.

In this connection it is proper to state that the National Government must always have through the Tariff substantially as much income as at this time, and consequently a vast number of tariff schedules must be made with only partial or no regard to protection, and must bring in many times more revenue than the application of the protective principle only would secure.

These two requirements of protection as the minimum and revenue as the maximum, give the utmost margin for just and right determination of maximum and minimum schedules, and the safeguarding both of the national weal and that of each particular industry.[1]

Confining ourselves to the protective principle, we find many schedules—some of them upon the prime necessities of life—returning the Government no revenue of consequence, and yet under the claims of the protective theory, bearing a tariff schedule—not merely equal to the difference in the cost of

[1] This was written in 1907, before we had the income tax. Prior to the adoption of the income tax the bulk of the revenue of the United States came from customs and "internal revenue" which was derived chiefly from excise taxes on tobacco and alcoholic beverages. In 1907, the year the Miles report was written, the customs revenue constituted one-half the total revenue of the United States: $332,233,000 out of a total revenue of $665,860,000. Since the adoption of the income tax, the tariff has ceased to be a significant source of revenue. Thus, in 1948 customs receipts yielded $421,723,000 out of a total revenue of $44,745,542,000, less than one per cent of the total.

[23]

production here and abroad, with all reasonable contingencies allowed for—but decidedly in excess of the total wage cost of production in this country.

We find some of these schedules many times in excess of "the difference between the cost of production here and abroad". We find that individuals who are at the top, both in stock holdings and in management in some of these same industries, declare privately that these schedules are wrong, and that the best interest of those industries themselves, as well as the interests of the country at large, require adjustment at the earliest possible moment. They say that now is the time for revision, while the country is so prosperous that adjustment may easily be made to new conditions.

We find, too, that there are more or less of these inequalities in almost every direction and every industry. Out of 77 industries tabulated by us, there is scarcely one but has some members who declare for readjustment on the grounds here stated of injustice and inequality. These statements by themselves might well make our radical revisionist friends more radical; but your Committee has declarations from men, who can no more be questioned than those above referred to, to the effect that many others of our schedules are as low as in reason they ought to be.

In two great industries, for instance, we are credibly informed that the lower grades of their products, being those that are made mostly by machinery, with the minimum either of hand or skilled labor, can now be produced in this country substantially as cheaply as anywhere in the world, and there is consequently no need of protection thereon. On the other hand, the high grade wares, requiring the finest touch and most artistic handling, are already in our own markets in very severe competition with the foreign product, for the reason that the most skilled artisan and the artist work for much less compensation abroad than here.

We submit to our Revisionist Members that the interests alike of the manufacturers named, and of the country at large, require us to support these industries in the maintenance of such schedules at no lower level than that which now obtains. These various conditions make it clear to your Committee that the present Tariff is in great need of revision, but only schedule by schedule—some to be lowered in various degrees; others not to be lowered at all.

Of those members who have replied to our inquiries upon this subject out of a total of 1,800 members, 350, or 20 per cent, are radically opposed to revision; 8 per cent are opposed to it at this time on grounds of expediency, lest it unsettle business, etc.; 55 per cent want revision—most of them of a radical kind, but one-fifth of them wanting only partial revision; 17 per cent are indifferent or uninformed, or not entitled to vote. Those decidedly wanting revision now, or in the near future, are, therefore, twice those who are either decidedly opposed to revision, or opposed to it for the time being. Taken by industries, out of 77 different industries tabulated, 56 vote for revision, casting a total of 1,510 votes, 16 industries vote against revision, casting a total of 102 votes; 5 industries are each tied in their votes, casting a total of 28 votes.[2]

A TARIFF COMMISSION

One of the most interesting developments of our inquiry is the clear disclosure that our members are overwhelmingly in favor of a Tariff Commission, with semi-judicial powers, as, for example, to summon witnesses; this commission to investigate thoroughly and scientifically the various schedules, and from time to time submit their conclusions in the form of recommendations to Congress and the Executive.

Out of 1,384 members who have expressed their wishes on this question, 1,221 are for a Tariff Commission, and 153 are opposed to a Commission. The number in favor of a Tariff Commission is just eight times the number of those opposed. One-half of our Stand Pat members vote in favor of a Tariff Commission. Taken by industries, 76 are favorable to a commission casting a total of 1,381 votes; only one industry is opposed, casting only one vote.

---

[2] Here Miles displayed his genius for handling conflicting interests. He pioneered in what has now become a common democratic procedure by taking a referendum of the membership of the Manufacturers' Association and obtained an overwhelming vote against existing tariff rates among the chief beneficiaries of protection.

We interpret this as evidence of the fairness of our Stand Pat members, and their confidence that a high-minded, impartial, and well-informed tribunal—acting with that degree of intelligence and honor which governs a court—will protect them in their present schedules.

Of the few who oppose a Tariff Commission, many do it because of the character of previous commissions, who, in their belief, were subservient to private interests, and therefore incompetent and inefficient; but we emphasize the fact that the Commission now contemplated would be not unlike the Interstate Commerce Commission; would be as free from reproach, pull and secret influence, and would take the Tariff up and out of politics and make its determinations like those of a court. Secretary Root has said that the Governmental control which the people deem just and necessary they will have. They are coming clearly to see that the control of the Tariff, to be just, must of necessity be a semi-judicial and not a political control.

Not one civil case in forty thousand tried before our courts to-day so vitally affects the pockets and the welfare of the people, as does each and every Tariff Schedule. A hundred years ago judges upon the bench showed the grossest partiality, and were in every way affected by special influence. Our tariff makers are in just that position at this time. We have not appreciated the situation. Those things are permitted in the making of Tariff Schedules which would ruin our civilization or bring about revolution if practiced by our courts. The same standard should prevail in the one case as in the other. . . .

The great mass of our people must be able to go quietly about their daily affairs in full confidence that any tariff case presented to a Commission, with whatever measure of personal influence and special zeal, will be considered with as perfect regard of the rights and the welfare of each other interest and of the general public, as if such other interests were directly and personally represented. This is the feeling our people have with reference to our courts and all judicial hearings. We have the same sense of security with reference to Railroad Rate Legislation and our Interstate Commerce Commission. Such well-advised security marks the measure of our civilization. That certainly must prevail, and rightly so, with reference to tariff determinations.

Under the present system it is a matter of common knowledge that the Tariff Rate depends largely upon the influence at Washington of the interest affected. Those not active at Washington, but attending to their business in the accustomed ways, are without anything like adequate consideration. They are not protected. One of the most prominent men in public affairs, who, himself, is in a measure both judge and jury in the making of Tariff schedules, is as truthful as he is blunt in saying: "Why of course, if any of the fellows down in my district should want a certain schedule, I would work for it. You wouldn't expect anything else, would you? It is a practical matter and I work for my district."

One of the ablest members of the Republican party in the Senate said recently: "Congress is really not competent to revise the Tariff." A representative like the one quoted may be big enough for his district; he is not big enough for his country. Our country is too large; our independence too delicate for us to permit with safety any other than a most high-minded, judicial and scientific determination of Tariff Schedules. Resolutions favoring a Tariff Commission will be offered through the customary channel.

RECIPROCITY

As said recently by Secretary Root: "A single, straight-out Tariff was all right in a world of single, straight-out Tariffs, but we have passed on during the course of years, into a world, for the most part, of maximum and minimum Tariffs; and with our single rate Tariff, we are left with very little to defend ourselves from bad treatment. Every country in the world can put up its Tariff against our products, as compared with similar products from other countries, without suffering, so far as our present law is concerned. Every country in the world knows that if it puts down the rate on our products in its Tariff, it will get no benefit from it, because we have to charge the same rate to that country that we do to the country which treats us the worst in respect to Tariff rates."

We are the greatest manufacturing nation upon earth. The protective policy has vastly helped us to this situation. It must not now be turned against us, but must be adapted to present-day conditions. Those who framed the last Tariff law saw this clearly, and provided for Reciprocal Agreements, purposely putting the Tariff so high that, in their own belief, it was justified only upon the basis of Reciprocal Agreements. We owe no debt of gratitude to those who purposely have made of no avail the negotiation of Reciprocity Treaties, as contemplated and provided for in the Tariff Bill itself. By reciprocity and truly protective duties, we will protect our trade abroad as well as at home, and greatly enlarge our foreign markets.

Of 1,260 members who have expressed themselves upon this subject, 1,040 are for reciprocity; 220 are opposed. The proportion in favor is as 5 to 1. A resolution favorable to reciprocity will be submitted through the usual channels.

OUR FUTURE WORK. Of 1,307 members answering our question, whether they desire this Association to collect facts and information and continue the investigation—1,250 say, "Yes", and 57 "No". Of the latter, some feel that the work should be done by each interest separately and without reference to others. The expression as favorable to a continuance of the work is in the proportion of 20 to 1.

It is to be borne in mind that we, collectively, represent only the manufacturing interests of this country. The Tariff is particularly to our benefit. There are countless millions who do not so directly feel the benefits. We must take them into consideration and not expect a settlement satisfactory only to ourselves to obtain, nor that what is moderately satisfactory to ourselves, is satisfactory to the nation at large. Such inequalities and injustice as exist in the Tariff Schedules must be taken out if only because of the popular demand. These inequalities are as a mote in the public eye. They must be removed, or injustice of the opposite kind may be the consequence. The leaders in Washington, Stand Pat and all, have virtually promised revision after the Presidential election, and as conservative business men, it behooves us to help make that revision just and equitable. Our Association has, as you know, consistently and persistently, for years, stood for Tariff Revision and Reciprocity. The time for action is now upon us. In the language of Burke: "We have a State to preserve, as well as a State to reform."

Your Committee believes that high-minded, non-partisan action, as recommended, would bring about a gradual, intelligent revision of the Tariff without disturbance of business conditions.

Tariff agitation of the old kind must always bring distress, because it is unreasonable, illogical, unfair and beyond calculation. It is for us now to help to determine whether distress of this kind shall again and periodically come upon our country, or the matter forever be sanely and helpfully disposed of by the establishment of a proper Commission.

TIME FOR REVISION: The time for revision is of small importance, as against the Method of Revision. It is time now and to-day that any party or set of men, supposed to safeguard its honor and the welfare of the country, give ample and unquestionable assurance that revision will come as soon as practicable, and that the revision will be of the right sort, and not at all after the previous fashion. We have been deceived by promises, and promise-makers must now give some surety with their promises.

The National Administration is, we believe, pledged to the general policy here recommended. Let the present Convention with Germany be enforced, other like conventions be framed, and let the party wishing our respect or our suffrage find a way of making a promise now and at once, with conduct to match, day after day, that our tariff will be cared for, as here outlined, at the earliest practicable moment. Much legislation can be accomplished in the coming Congress, and the good faith or bad faith evidenced in that legislation will measure the confidence that may be placed in party promises and Members of Congress.

LASTLY: A Tariff Schedule is after all a PRICE, a measure of difference, and of value. What one of us but has changed his prices, not once but a hundred times since 1897. Change in prices to meet changing conditions is a necessity in business. Change; reasonable, natural logical change, makes for life and growth. Only the figures on our Tariff Sheets are dead and changeless. They are the highest ever and not reasonable. May they too, soon partake of life, and change, and reason.

(Signed)

> H. E. MILES *(Chairman)*
> W. H. PARLIN,
> JOHN E. MCINTOSH,
> E. H. DEAN,
> WM. A. VAWTER.

The Miles report met with an enthusiastic reception at the 12th Annual Convention of the National Association of Manufacturers and the following resolution was adopted on May 22, 1907.

Resolved, That the National Association of Manufacturers declares itself in favor of a revision of the Tariff at the earliest practicable date and the making of treaties of reciprocity meantime as originally provided for by the present tariff laws.

Whereas, the members of the National Association of Manufacturers have by correspondence expressed themselves in the proportion of 8 to 1 that to secure a thoroughly intelligent revision of the tariff laws there should be established a nonpartisan tariff commission not unlike the present Interstate Commerce Commission, with semi-judicial powers, as for example to summon witnesses, this commission to investigate thoroughly and scientifically the various schedules and from time to time submit their conclusions in the form of recommendations to Congress and the Executive.

Therefore, Be it Resolved, that the National Association of Manufacturers formally declares itself in favor of such a commission and hereby instructs its officers to make every reasonable endeavor to secure the appointment of such a permanent Commission at the earliest possible date.

Miles took this resolution as a mandate and having been re-elected Chairman of the Tariff Committee of the Association, he set his course. Using prohibitive tariff rates, in which the Dingley Tariff abounded, as illustrations of Congressional incompetence and subservience to special interests, he concentrated on his demand for the creation of a Tariff Commission as the only means of bringing about an honest tariff, scientifically arrived at by a competent impartial body.

In letters to numerous correspondents and addresses before meetings of industrial and business associations he hammered away on this point. He won over President Roosevelt and Secretary Taft whose Presidential star was just rising over the political horizon.

He established contact with some of the Progressive Republican senators, especially La Follette and Beveridge. Writing to Beveridge on October 2, 1907, he said in the concluding paragraphs of a long letter:

> The present situation is simply unendurable. The Standpatters propose by specious talk . . . to hold the present situation over the next election and then give us the old sort of revision. If by any chance they should do all this, the people would rebel against that revision and that tariff would have to be made over, in my judgment, within twelve or twenty-four months.

> Substantially the manufacturers are Republicans as well as Protectionists. They have no end of information showing that the Republican Party has sold out the consuming public, that is, the whole country, every time in our generation that it has made a tariff. We do not want to publish that information.[3]

Beveridge having been won over to the idea of a Tariff Commission, with his characteristic impetuosity introduced a bill in the Senate in January 1908 for the creation of a Tariff Commission without previous understanding with Miles. Claude G. Bowers in his biography of Senator Beveridge reports that in the preparation of his speech in support of the bill,

> Beveridge, with his genius for research, was mobilizing facts, intended for the public generally as much as for the Senate. He postponed the date for its delivery until in February and sent Miles an explanation: 'This will give opportunity for your delegation to visit the President and Congress; and if you get a rebuke from the Speaker or Mr. Aldrich, as may be the case, this speech, and what I hope will be your reception of it, will show that you are in earnest and not to be rebuffed.[4]

---

[3] Claude G. Bowers; Beveridge and the Progressive Era, p. 271.

[4] Bowers, p. 273; A detailed account of Beveridge's conversion to the idea of a Tariff Commission and the part he played is given by Bowers on pp. 269–277.

Miles opened his 1908 campaign with an article entitled "Why Manufacturers Want Tariff Revision" in the January issue of the North American Review, at that time the leading and perhaps most influential magazine in the country, edited by "the maker of Presidents", George Harvey. He set forth the now familiar principle of protection as measured by the difference between costs in this and competing foreign countries and cited many illustrations of prohibitive rates greatly exceeding not only the difference in cost but the entire cost of production in the United States. He made the bold assertion that

> in many cases they exceeded this difference between the cost of manufacture abroad and that at home from five to a thousand times.[5]

He gave a novel definition of protection, certainly one never heard from a protectionist:

> protection is two-edged; the manufacturer must be protected and so must the consumer. This latter fact has been largely overlooked. Combination, in replacing competition, has taken protection away from the consumer. What was right ten years ago (before the organization of the combines) is not right today.[6]

He concluded the article with an appeal for

> a Tariff Commission without favor and without fear; a commission empowered to examine in detail every trust and every industry asking for a protective tariff; a commission which will not seek to confound but enlighten; a commission capable of considering national and international needs and ethics. . . .[7]

> The establishment of a Tariff Commission at the coming session of Congress would take the tariff out of politics, preclude any possible unfavorable agitation . . . and when at

---

[5] North American Review, January 1908, p. 36.
[6] id. p. 42.
[7] id. p. 44.

last Revision does come, instead of 'monkeying' and 'tinkering' of the past it will be wholly sane and fair.[8]

The pressure brought to bear by Miles and Sanders through their organizations coupled with the introduction of the Beveridge bill forced Speaker Cannon and Chairman Sereno E. Payne of the Ways and Means Committee to hold a hearing on the subject of a Permanent Tariff Commission on February 4, 1908. Those appearing and speaking at the hearing were marshalled by President James W. Van Cleave of the National Association of Manufacturers and represented exclusively industrial, agricultural and commercial interests. Representatives of the consuming public were conspicuous by their absence.

Miles came to the meeting loaded with facts and figures showing the iniquities and monstrosities of the tariff. But when called upon to speak, he made a mild, courteous appeal for the creation of a Tariff Commission which would be charged with the duty of getting at the facts and thereby relieve the overworked members of the Ways and Means Committee who had so many other duties to perform. The others spoke in a similar vein.

After all the speeches had been made, Speaker Cannon delivered a reply in which he ridiculed the idea of a Tariff Commission, expressed the conviction that there was not "a man in the United States, who knows as much of the schedules and who is as well equipped for that work" as Sereno Payne. The hearing was a fizzle and Miles made this entry in his copy of the hearings:

"As I entered the room President Van Cleve drew me aside and said Speaker Cannon had just promised to meet our demands if we would not *attack* Congress as we had planned. As Van Cleve was my superior officer and very earnest in requesting that I would *not* speak forthright as planned, I spoke softly and, in effect, foolishly.

Almost immediately after, we saw that Cannon lied to get us out of town without revelations."

[8] id. p. 45.

If Cannon and Payne thought that their manoeuvre would stop the movement for a Tariff Commission they underestimated Miles' earnest interest in the cause he had espoused and the forces he had set in motion. The fiasco of the hearing served only to whip Miles to redoubled effort. He set to work on a scorching exposé of Payne's ways of tariff-making, using the facts cited by Payne himself in his chapter in the book "The Making of America". He put it in a pamphlet called: "The Old Way and the Right Way; Remarkable Statements of Hon. Sereno E. Payne, Chairman of the Ways and Means Committee".

Irked by President Roosevelt's failure to come out publicly for a Tariff Commission, although privately he had repeatedly assured Miles that he was heart and soul with him, he wrote the President on February 21, 1908, little more than a fortnight after the Cannon-Payne meeting, that if the standpatters had their way, the Republican party might go down in defeat in the coming Presidential election. Claude Bowers in his book on Beveridge thus sums up the contents of a letter Miles wrote to Roosevelt:

> It was too bad that some of the standpatters are likely to insist upon our proving them before the whole people arrant cowards and knaves, but if they insist, it was their feast or funeral. Would the President look over the enclosed pamphlet, which would be published in a few days, on how tariffs had been made and on the part Payne had played in making them?[9]
> "A few days later", says Bowers, "the pamphlet was in the mails speeding to the four corners."

We can do no more than give here a few extracts from that pamphlet to illustrate the plain speaking which marked his assault on the entrenched Congressional leaders of the Republican party which shocked their sensibilities as an act of lèse majesté.

Congressman Payne contributes a chapter on the tariff and the trusts in a work just issued, called "The Making of Amer-

[9] Claude G. Bowers; Beveridge etc. p. 275.

ica". Mr. Payne has taken part in the making of at least three or four tariffs and surely can speak, if any one can, as to the way tariffs have been made in this country. He substantially declares that if a Tariff Commission, after years of labor and investigation of costs in the places of production themselves, should lay the truth before him, he would "compromise" and make his deals regardless of the commission or its recommendations.

In this article Mr. Payne selects, as a choice example of a trust and the tariff "The Sugar Refineries Co.", commonly known as the Sugar Trust. He says:

It was a trust pure and simple. Its organizers expressed the purpose, among other things, to 'keep the price of sugar as low as consistent with reasonable profit' and generally to promote the interests of the parties hereto in all lawful and suitable ways'.

Mr. Payne continues:

They did endeavor 'generally to promote the interests of the parties hereto' with a vengeance, but they evidently did not keep the price of sugar 'as low as was consistent with reasonable profit'. Notwithstanding the enormous watering of stock, dividends unheard of before were declared and paid. As the product of this combination was a necessity of life required by every class of people the excessive profits demanded soon called the attention of the people to the existence of this monopoly. . . . The object in forming the sugar schedule of the tariff in 1890, and again in 1897, was to learn as nearly as possible the exact cost of refining sugar, and then to adjust the tariff so as to protect the labor interests and no more. Investigation into this subject proved very irksome and troublesome. It was impossible to get at the exact facts, as the experts were not inclined to reveal the secrets of their business to the Committee on Ways and Means. Different statements were made as to the cost of refining by different refineries, and then the best that could be done was a compromise rate for the differential duty between raw and refined sugar. . . . Enormous profits and extravagant divi-

dends forced from the people for a common necessity of
life have rightly earned for this particular trust widespread and just condemnation.

Think of it! A man who had to do with the last three tariffs
declares that the last tariff gave the sugar people protection
without adequate proof, and that his committee was unable
to get proof from the very men who stood before them demanding protection and having in their possession all possible proof. It is a reflection upon any industry that demands
protection and in the same breath refuses to justify its demands,
and an infinite reflection upon our representatives in Congress
that they ever compromise with such an interest.

Moreover, how great and good and thoughtful of the public
interest was Mr. Payne when, recently, he turned away representatives of the chief manufacturing and agricultural interests of the United States and with his best politician's voice
spoke of the necessity he felt of trusting no Tariff Commission
or other experts, even to help him in any measure to get his
information and secure the people's rights.

'No', said Mr. Payne, 'when my committee makes a tariff,
we must get our information 'at first ha-and'. Very rhetorical
and brave it sounded. His first ha-and dicker with the Sugar
Trust has cost the people of the United States two hundred
million dollars in the past ten years. Shall his insistence on
another 'first ha-and' proposition cost the people another two
hundred million dollars on a single item of the thousands
covered by the tariff?

The pamphlet cited other glaring examples of tariff favors to the
oil, steel and other monopolized industries and continued:

Says Mr. Payne: 'There are trusts in all countries, especially
in Germany and in free-trade England.' Mr. Payne seems not
to know that a trust in England must be as good in fact, as
American trusts are in their prospectuses. They must make their
money by their economies. They must sell at the lowest prices
that obtain anywhere in the world. If they get above the lowest international price, foreign competition immediately checks
their advance. In Germany, trusts do as in this country, they

add all that they can to the price and take every advantage of protection as of all other opportunities.

The price of steel to the German consumer is about the same as in this country, and for the same reason—a trust. On steel plates, however, the price in Germany is as low as anywhere in the world, even in free-trade England, and why? Because steel plates are on the free list and the German trust must meet the international and lowest prices, because of the open market. . . . Not old schedules[10] but honest schedules is today's demand. No longer shall ninety million people be subject to loose and careless action, vitally affecting their material interests. . . . President Roosevelt, Governor Hughes, Secretary Root, Secretary Taft and all other constructive statesmen know that this situation can not long continue. . . .

Imagine, if you can, a tariff framed in a know-it-all-in-ninety days session of a lot of novices under the direction of Mr. Payne and Mr. Dalzell of Pittsburgh. Not one of the Committee is a manufacturer, they know as little about manufacturing as manufacturers know about law, and yet Messrs. Payne, Dalzell and a very few others who support them insist that these men shall legislate as to affect the prices, cost of living and the profits and the savings of over ninety million people and shall determine what shall be our success in foreign trade. . . . As well give the throttle of a locomotive to a child and expect the best consequences.

It is with keenest regret that we note the absolute insistence of the standpatters that there be disclosures like these. It is infinitely for the public interest that they yield at once and save scandal. . . .

It is a great misfortune that men like Mr. Payne are allowed to call themselves Protectionists. They have been advanced by powerful interests not that the country may have protection but that a sleeping and trustful public may be wronged by the misapplication of the principle and its gross abuse. . . . The public is fast getting ready to care for itself in this matter without regard to obstructionists, active or passive.

---

[10] A pun directed at Payne who was nicknamed "Old Schedules".

Miles thus brought into the open President Roosevelt's name as a sponsor of the movement for a Tariff Commission, after letting him see the pamphlet before its publication. The substance of the pamphlet was also published in the March 15 issue of American Industries, the official organ of the National Association of Manufacturers.

The next issue of American Industries, April 1, 1908, opened with a strong article by Miles, "The Demand for a Tariff Commission". It displayed in the center of the first page a portrait of President Roosevelt under which appeared this legend:

"President Theodore Roosevelt. A consistent and fearless advocate of tariff adjustment upon whose initiative the present widespread demand for the creation by Congress of a Tariff Commission was inaugurated". The second page had a portrait of "Secretary William H. Taft, whose public and private attitude in favor of an equable adjustment of the tariff has given aid and encouragement to the friends and advocates of a Tariff Commission."

The article contained several additional disclosures of the old back-stage ways of tariff-making and emphasized that the proposed Tariff Commission "must be reasonably independent in its investigation . . . and must have power to summon witnesses and compel the disclosure of costs and other data."

In the May 1 issue Miles in an article on "The Tariff Situation Today" gave an account "of the campaign for honest tariff schedules." He followed it up with "An Open Letter to Secretary Taft" taking issue with a statement made by Mr. Taft in a newspaper interview in which he was quoted as saying: "I should like to see such a Commission in successful operation, but the truth is Congress will never accept the conclusions of a Commission on the tariff."

[38]

Miles closed his letter with these words:

This last and greatest of the grafts is going to be checked. The Dingley bill is not protective—it was not when made, for the reason that neither the principle you name nor any other principle except graft and grab had influence in its making.

The same issue contained the text of the bill introduced by Senator Robert M. La Follette in the Senate on March 20 for the creation of a Tariff Commission. It did not differ from the Beveridge Bill in its objective but went into much greater detail in outlining the duties and powers of the Commission.

The fierce publicity campaign conducted uninterruptedly by Miles throughout the months of January, February, March and April while Congress was in session, coupled with the pressure exercised by Beveridge, La Follette and the other Progressive Republican senators and the quiet backing by the President, finally led Aldrich to agree to a compromise measure. In his annual report to the thirteenth annual meeting of the National Association of Manufacturers held in New York on May 18–20, 1908, Miles was able to state that

The Senate of the United States on May sixteenth accepted in substance the views we hold and passed a resolution providing for the employment of experts who shall at once proceed to the investigation of classifications and rates and who "are especially directed to report what further legislation is necessary to secure equable treatment (reciprocity) for the agricultural and other products of the United States in foreign countries, and they shall also, in consideration of changes of rates, secure *proof* of the relative *cost of production* in this and in principal competing foreign countries of the various articles affected by the tariff upon which changes in the rates of duties are desirable." It was interesting to your Committee in this connection to hear from one of the ablest statesmen and staunchest protectionists in America that this resolution is the first recognition by either branch of Congress of the underlying principle of international costs as properly determining each particular rate.

While this fell far short of an independent commission as proposed in the Beveridge and La Follette bills, the requirement of "proof of the relative cost of production" was a distinct concession to the demands made by Miles.

In reviewing the work of the year, Miles said:

The substantial difference between the work of the past year and of previous years is found in the insistence of this Committee that your judgment should be made clear to the country and receive practical attention by the law-making powers. In consequence of this effort, the tariff has come to be seen with new eyes by all the people. Never again will a tariff be made in the uncertain and slipshod methods of the past. More and more will the rates themselves square with the underlying principles. These underlying principles have been repeatedly affirmed by the President of the United States; and by the leading candidates for the Presidency. They have recently for the first time been made an important part of the tariff planks in many state platforms.

As we shall see, Miles was overoptimistic in predicting that "never again" would the old slipshod methods of tariff-making be resorted to. The disappointment was to come within a few months.

Miles dwelt on the subject of reciprocity in the following remarks in his report at the annual meeting:

RECIPROCITY

Eight years ago, in the convention of 1900, we demanded reciprocity upon the lines originally contemplated and provided for in the present law. Exhaustive examination shows that while the House did not provide for reciprocity in its original bill, the duties were in the Committee of Conference purposely made high enough to provide protection upon the basis of twenty per cent reductions in reciprocal agreements.

There were very many differences in rates between the original House and the Senate Bills, and in the great majority of these cases the Conference Committee accepted the higher figures. In some cases a compromise figure, very seldom the lower figure.

The language of the law is explicit. As Senator Dolliver said the rates were made high for the purpose of trading them off.

President McKinley said upon entering the Presidency that the great success of his Administration would lie largely in the making of reciprocal treaties and the increase of our foreign trade. It was a matter of regret and mortification to him that unfortunate influences practically vitiated this provision of the law, and defeated his expectations.

Had large and intelligent use been made of reciprocity during the last ten years we would now see no smokeless chimneys, and fewer idle operatives. Of all the great nations we have stood aloof, refused to negotiate, and been unable through a Tariff Commission or other body of experts even to receive intelligently and with due consideration the proposals of nations who wish to treat with us.

Of an annual output of manufactures valued at $15,000,000,000, we export only about five per cent and if from this amount we deduct such nearly crude manufactures as copper, petroleum and its products, iron and steel in bars, pigs and rails, we have an export of the more highly finished products of only about three per cent of our total manufacturers. As has been said, America is little more than a huge stevedore bearing down to the ships of the sea crude and semi-crude materials for the use of foreign manufacturers.

Not only this, but from the wilfulness of ignorance or selfishness American manufacturers have been forced to build factories in Canada. Our miscalled protection has taken employment away from American laborers and given it to Canadians, not only to supply Canadian markets but that goods formerly manufactured in this country may now be made in Canadian factories to supply France and other foreign territories, under the reciprocal treaties of Canada.

In his report he did not forget to pay his respects to the principal count in his indictment of the tariff—the fostering of monopoly:

Seven years ago our disbelief in the present tariff was evidenced by our formal declaration that a tariff should 'furnish adequate protection to such products only as require it, without providing the opportunity for monopoly abuses."

Monopoly is a word we need not fear to use, the above resolution makes no objection to doing big things in big ways. It notes only this—that when monopolies are formed they shall not be aided, abetted or enriched by Congress and the President of the United States through the tariff.

Just government uses its powers for the protection and guidance of the weak, rather than for the increase of the power of the powerful. It is necessary that no great manufacturing or commercial aggregation be unjustly favored by a governmentally enforced and hourly contribution of Peter's pence from the poor and the powerless. It is necessary to the well-being of ourselves as manufacturers that the principle of protection upon which we justly depend, shall not be degraded to this use, and equally that there shall be no suspicion of such degradation.

OUR COMMON INTEREST

It has been said that our Association should not interest itself in the tariff on the ground that the interest of the members are antagonistic. We do not so find. To us protection is a sacred principle. Protection is necessary that our people may be economically free. It is voted to us by the people as a trust to be measured out to us in the tariff by Congress, the oath-bound servant of the people, with intelligence in just and equal measure, and to be used by us only in ways conducive to the public good.

Congress and the Administration in the continuance of the present tariff for long years with full knowledge of its unfairness, have permitted, if not invited, manufacturers to consolidate and by consolidation to add no inconsiderable part of certain unfair schedules to their selling prices.

Your committee sought for long months to use only soft speech and gentle ways. It found in Congress, backed by immeasurable power, a few men representing each his own constituency only, not caring how a tariff over-favorable to his constituency affects the rest of the United States. In these men is the sum total of oppositions to our propositions. These men insist on again legislating not for the nation, but for their respective constituencies only.

Not less than $7,000,000,000 annually of our manufacturers being one-half of the total is over-charged to the consumers because the tariff was made in great measure by such men as these and has been permitted to continue without change by Congress and the Administration. A plea of ignorance will not blot out the figures. It is a question if such a plea will palliate the moral impropriety.

The Miles report was signed by all the members of the Tariff Committee except one, a Mr. Dean. It was natural that this outspoken criticism of the tariff should meet with disapproval in a body consisting of manufacturers of so many varied industries enjoying tariff protection. Mr. Dean was the spokesman of the dissenters. As soon as Miles concluded the reading of his report, Mr. Dean asked for the floor to submit his minority report. Referring to the tariff, Mr. Dean said:

No tariff commission can take this question out of party politics. . . . I believe it to be the wrong policy for this great Association of Manufacturers to enter into party politics. . . . It can not be done without great dissensions, loss of membership and loss of revenue. It is not an issue on which we can expect to reach an agreement or even compromise. . . .

The articles published in American Industries and other publications of the National Association in advocating tariff reduction have been most discourteous to the present administration. The attacks made on the Speaker of the House, the Chairman of the Ways and Means Committee and on Congressman Dalzell for not dropping into line have been unjust and abusive. Charges of Congressional incompetency and crookedness in connection with tariff rates have been freely made, but unsubstantiated by any evidence. The whole attempt of the Association to browbeat Congress into a scheme for immediate tariff reduction has been tactless and offensive. . . . While there are many members of this Association who favor tariff revision, I think the great majority are opposed to general revision. . . . Many use (the term) when they mean tariff reduction always having in mind a reduction of duties, and no idea of increasing rates. . . .

After citing statistics of the growth of our foreign commerce under the Dingley tariff, Mr. Dean said: "With these splendid results why enter into the doubtful experiment of instituting a Tariff Commission?"

His statement precipitated a lively debate on both sides of the question. The debate was concluded with statements by President Van Cleave, who supported Mr. Miles, and by Miles himself, with the result that the resolution introduced by Mr. Miles was passed with only one dissenting vote, presumably Mr. Dean's. The resolution reiterated the demand for tariff revision and a Tariff Commission, contained in the resolution passed by the 1907 convention.

With renewed enthusiasm Miles continued his struggle. 1908 was a Presidential year with Taft's nomination a foregone conclusion. Miles was determined to get Taft's commitment to tariff revision with the aid of a Tariff Commission. Also for an appropriate plank in the Republican platform. Less than a month after the close of the annual meeting of the Manufacturer's Association, he wrote to me in a letter dated June 16, 1908:

"I have been in Chicago a good deal of the time on the platform matter. I believe that we are going to get nothing more than a declaration for Revision upon the basis of international costs. These last words being my short way of saying the difference of cost of production here and abroad. Also declaration for maximum and minimum schedules.

I did think with you that we ought to fight very hard for a Commission or the employment of experts. I am afraid if we should, we would not get it and might not benefit our position.

I have a good understanding with Attorney General Wade Ellis, Columbus, Ohio, Mr. Taft's platform bearer. When I pressed him he said impatiently, "Oh, I know all about the thievery in the Tariff."

I am advised if we get this principle in the platform we can then stand on that and fight for the means necessary to make the Principle effective. Mr. Ellis' eyes glinted in a very interesting way when I said, "We will not be willing again to see a President sign a dishonest, unscientific tariff on the plea of ignorance." I believe if we get this plank, as I am sure we will, and then put great stress upon the point seldom, if ever, made, that the President is substantially as responsible when he signs it as Congress for making it, we will find ourselves travelling down the middle of the road with much success."

Miles' forecast of the Republican platform proved accurate. On June 18, the Republican convention meeting in Chicago adopted the following tariff plank:

"In all tariff legislation the true principle of protection is best maintained by the imposition of such duties as will equal the difference between the cost of production at home and abroad together with a reasonable profit to American industry. We favor the establishment of maximum and minimum rates to be administered by the President under limitations fixed in the law, the maximum to be available to meet discrimination by foreign countries against American goods entering their markets and the minimum to represent the normal measure of protection at home."[11]

In his speech of acceptance delivered in Cincinnati July 28, Candidate Taft gave added emphasis to the new formula, when, referring to the Dingley Tariff, he said:

"The tariff in a number of schedules exceeds the difference between the cost of production of such articles abroad and at home, including a reasonable profit to the American producer. The excess over that difference serves no useful purpose, but

---

[11] N. Y. Times, June 19, 1908.

offers a temptation to those who would monopolize the production and the sale of such articles in this country, to profit by the excessive rate. . . ."

He pledged the Republican party to revision of the tariff at a special session of Congress "upon the incoming of the new Administration".[12]

Miles' achievement established a new milestone in the formulation of tariff protection. Important as it was, however, it fell short of the other goal he had set for himself,—the establishment of a Tariff Commission. As he indicated in his letter of June 16, quoted above, his fight for a Tariff Commission had just begun, and was to continue after the election.

In the meantime, yielding to the entreaties of his wife to take a much needed rest from his strenuous activities, he agreed to go for a vacation to England. On his way from Racine to the steamer he conceived the idea that that would be a wonderful opportunity to meet British leaders in industry and Government and get their views on the effect of the tariff on the commerce between the two countries, and perhaps secure their cooperation in facilitating comparisons of costs of production in England and the United States. The projected "rest" turned into even more strenuous activity aiming to cover much ground in a short interval of less than two months. He even extended his trip beyond England by going to Paris to speak before the American Chamber of Commerce and get leads on our relations with France. Writing from London on August 4, 1908, he said:

"You will be pleased to hear that the Congress for Freer International Trade opened today successfully. It has enabled me to make the acquaintance of many able and splendid men who will help our tariff work exceedingly, if I may judge this soon. I have just spent 4½ hours with Sir William Holland,

[12] N. Y. Times, July 29, 1908.

who is in the woolens. He has given me the choicest refer-
ences to tin plate manufacturers, steel, cotton, woolen, plate
glass, and will gladly add any others I later request. I have,
therefore, great hopes of coming home with abundant information on international costs, that will interest and help all concerned. Two other Members of Parliament have interested
themselves equally and I consequently feel that we are in the
way to get results."

No sooner was he off the boat in New York on September 1st
than he went into conference with President Van Cleave on plans
for the campaign. Writing from Racine on September 9, he said:

"I think you will be happy to hear that President Van
Cleave and I are in splendid accord on the tariff policy and
certain features which disturbed me in New York have been
corrected.

It is our present intention to call the Executive Committee
together September 25 in the belief they will advocate an
aggressive tariff campaign which will compel the Republican
party, if they are to have the support of the manufacturers,
to make pledges not yet given and we hope to induce Mr.
Taft to make a constructive and definite statement on tariff-
making that will be as good as a creed. I am writing him today
thinking I may get an interview with him within a few days.

Of course, Executive Committees etc., called together some-
what unexpectedly may not think fast enough, but I believe we
will find in our large organization a Committee, each member
of which will be a positive force, leaving less to the person-
ality etc., of the Chairman and will at the same time be able
to make strong statements which will require Mr. Taft's attention. In general the situation looks to me better in these respects than any time since Taft's nomination. . . .

I hope to find time shortly to get out a statement with quotations from Cleveland, McKinley, Roosevelt and Taft, much in
line with our program heading it, "The Tariff and four Presidents", prompting Taft in a measure to be the fourth President in a worthy sense and make us less mindful than we now
are that "he wants the Presidency" and is thinking of little
else than getting it any way he may."

While acting boldly as a leader, Miles was aware of the danger of getting out of step with his following. Writing to me from Racine two days later, he had this to say:

"We must not do anything that will be interpreted as a desire to advance Bryan's cause. . . . The vast majority of the business interests of the United States thinking of the general business situation would rather chance any tariff and a thousand times rather chance our policy to restrain Payne and Dalzell and influence the Republicans after election, than take any chances on Democrats getting in and a frightful shock November 4 next to returning prosperity.

My solution is Grant's at the end of his first battle. He had been frightened to death all day; it then occurred to him his opponent had probably been as much frightened as he and he was never frightened afterwards.

Our opponents are as much frightened as we. They know our cause to be sound and right. We should go ahead pell-mell to victory. Our victory, the Republican victory, for Mr. Taft can immeasurably advance the Republican cause by fully, explicitly and constructively acknowledging our position."

The Democrats soon gave him the desired opportunity for making a public disavowal of any intention to support their party. The Democratic National Committee had attempted to make political capital by quoting his utterances criticizing Republican tariff making. He seized the occasion to show in an emphatic manner that he had no more confidence in Democratic ways of tariff making than he had in Republican. Writing in American Industries of November 1, 1908 he said:

When, after cheap and specious promises, such as they are now again making, the Democrats were given a chance (their only chance in our generation) to make a tariff, they gave us the Wilson bill, a measure so dishonest and unfair that their own President, Mr. Cleveland, pronounced it a tariff of 'perfidy and dishonor'. 'Bought, bought, bought' and refused to sign it. For money bribes and other considerations they gave the sugar trust a tariff which caused sugar stock to advance from 98⅞ to 106½ in a day or two. They gave Standard Oil the first protection it ever received—a protection that has enabled this trust to charge American consumers 35% to 45% more than foreign users, as shown by Government investigation.

He concluded with the statement that only a Tariff Commission of experts can put an end to these political practices.

In the midst of the Presidential campaign, apparently as an assurance to the people that the Republican party meant to live up to its platform promises, Sereno E. Payne, Chairman of the Ways and Means Committee, issued a public announcement that following the election his Committee would begin to hold hearings on November 10 with a view to tariff revision. Far from rejoicing and greeting the step as a triumph crowning his efforts of more than a year, Miles regarded Payne's action as a challenge to his program for a Tariff Commission. Writing to me on November 12, 1908 a few days after the election of Mr. Taft, he said:

"The average manufacturer who is interested in the tariff is almost appalled by Payne's audacity. It fairly stuns us. The question is whether to go out on the highway or cry aloud or what.

Do you think we ought to appear before this cut and dried, wretched committee now or let them have their foolish hearing and then use it as material against them a little later? The utter asininity of the testimony and everything else will afford splendid material, while if we go down there we will seem to acquiesce in Payne's proposition.

There are many ways of looking at this and so far I can not bring myself to think of going there, at least until I have heard from Mr. Taft."

He did hear from Mr. Taft not only privately, but also publicly.

As Mr. Payne opened his tariff hearings with Miles and his associates, conspicuous by their absence, President-elect Taft in a published newspaper interview was quoted as saying: "Where are the Members of the National Association of Manufacturers? Why have they not appeared? It seems to me they should present their side of the question now."

To this President Van Cleave replied in an article in the American Industries of December 1, 1908, in which he gave the reasons for their absence.

First, as it is composed of members representing nearly all the crafts in the country the Association can not, as an organization, have a direct interest in any particular schedules. . . .

The other and far more important reason why we have kept out is that we are opposed to this plan of making tariff investigations which are intended to be used as a groundwork for a readjustment of the duties. We are not opposed to the men making the inquiry, but are opposed to the system.

However, Miles felt he could not let Mr. Taft's challenge go unanswered. While Mr. Van Cleave took the position that the Manufacturer's Association as such could not speak officially at a tariff hearing because of divergent interests between different industries constituting the membership of the association, Miles made it a point to speak in his personal capacity, although reflecting the views of numerous industries.

When he finally appeared before the Committee on December 5th, 1908 he was true to form and by his outspoken criticism of the Tariff, coming, as it did, not from an academic free trader, but a manufacturer and avowed Republican and protectionist, he aroused and provoked the members of the Committee to so lively a discussion that the testimony filled 120 closely printed pages of the Committee's hearings.[13]

He hammered away on four main points in his testimony: 1) The Tariff favors the trusts at the expense not only of the ultimate con-

---

[13] Tariff Hearings before the Committees on Ways and Means of the House of Representatives. Sixtieth Congress 1908–09. Volume VII, pp. 7589–7710.

sumer, but of the great body of manufacturers who use the products made by the trusts; 2) the duties on trust-made goods are scandalously excessive; 3) no protection should be granted to any industry unless it submits conclusive proof that it needs it—"no proof—no protection"; 4) the need of a Tariff Commission.

1. TARIFF FAVORS THE TRUSTS. He defined a trust as any large corporation or combination of corporations which was able to control the market price of its products.

Speaking of the excessive protection granted to the trusts he cited as illustrations the duties on iron and steel, brass, lead, oil, rubber, plate glass and wool.

IRON AND STEEL. As an introduction to his own statement Miles quoted Carnegie, who, in a speech to steel manufacturers in 1884, said:

> "We are creatures of the tariff and if ever the steel manufacturers here attempt to control or have any general understanding among them the tariff would not exist one session of Congress. The theory of protection is that home competition will soon reduce the price of the product, so that it will yield only the usual profit. Any understanding among us would simply attempt to defeat this. There never has been and never will be such an understanding."[14]

Contrary to Carnegie's fears, expressed in 1884, said Miles, he lived to see the formation of the steel trust fifteen years later in which the Carnegie holdings underwent this fantastic financial transformation: Shortly before the formation of the U. S. Steel Corporation, the Carnegie Company's own book value was $81,000,000. Carnegie offered to acquire the Frick Company for which Frick asked $35,000,000. Frick finally sold out for $22,000,000 in cash in addition to a stock interest. The two companies, with 22 million

---

[14] Hearings p. 7596 (Quotation from American Manufacturer, July 25, 1884.)

dollars less assets, were consolidated at a value of $320,000,000. A few weeks later Carnegie sold the consolidated company to U. S. Steel at a cash valuation of $447,000,000.[15]

Miles proceeded to enlighten the Committee on the excessive rates on steel products. No wonder, he said, that with the aid of these tariff-rigged prices the water which was poured into the stock of the Steel Corporation turned into solid value from the swollen profits in the four years of operation of the Steel Company.[16]

Asked by members of the Committee what duties he would recommend for heavy steel products he had referred to, he said the maximum duty for trading purposes in reciprocity negotiations should be 15% and they should go on the free list on the minimum schedule.

OIL. He charged the Standard Oil Company with having adroitly put a joker in the Tariff Act which made the ostensibly duty free imported petroleum subject to duty when imported from any country levying a duty on oil. This resulted in the imposition of a 99% duty on Russian oil, the only oil available for export at that time outside the United States. It resulted in virtually shutting out all competition from foreign oil, while our exports exceeded 78 million dollars.[17]

Congressman Boutell (Rep.) remarked that the removal of the tariff on trust-controlled articles would result in the formation of international trusts. To this Miles replied that if the international trust fixed a uniformly high price all over the world the American implement manufacturer and other manufacturers would be again on a competitive basis with foreign manufacturers of the same products.[18] He taunted the Republican members of the Committee by

[15] Hearings, p. 7598–99.
[16] Hearings, p. 7599.
[17] Hearings, p. 7595.
[18] Hearings, p. 7647.

repeatedly referring to high prices of tariff-protected products as "Congress-made" prices.

Miles cited the case of the plate glass trust as a striking illustration of how the tariff on trust-made products works out as "permission from the U. S. Congress to raise prices" to the consumer. He quoted the President of the Pittsburg Plate Glass Company to the effect that the labor cost of making plate glass amounted to 48% of the selling price and was 50–70% higher in this country than in Europe, which would justify a duty of 24–34%. Instead, the tariff was fixed at 80% and the trust raised prices 100% within two years. It shared its windfall with labor by giving it one-sixth of the advances, five-sixths going to the company. Finally, said Miles,

"they made the American consumer pay nearly $2 for every $1 worth of glass he bought. They raised their prices so high that importers were able to pay the excessive tariff and bring plate glass in to advantage. Whereupon the plate-glass trust showed a new phase of trust management in writing importers that they must not bring in glass or they would be cut off from home supply upon such sizes as could not be imported to advantage, and the importers had to discontinue their effort to save the home consumer and advantage themselves, and leave that consumer wholly at the mercy of the trust upon an increase of price of 100 per cent."[19]

He cited several other trust-made products enjoying excessive protection, such as brass with a total cost of production of 17% of its selling price and a duty of 45% and annual exports of more than four million dollars; lead, with a cost of refining equal to 4% of its selling price and a tariff duty equivalent to 50–79%, or 10 to 20 times its total labor cost; linseed oil with a labor cost of 3% and an import duty of 50%; tobacco with a labor cost of 19% and a tariff equivalent to 147–153% of the selling price; the glucose

---

[19] Hearings, p. 7665.

trust producing starch at a labor cost of 11% and a duty equal to 46–69% of the selling price and glucose at a labor cost of 7% and a duty equal to 55%, enjoying an export trade of three million dollars as against total imports into the United States of $4,000.

Summing up that part of his testimony, he said:

"I am against Congress going into the trust business. . . . The tariff permits every trust in the United States to add a third to the selling price, and each trust adds that particular third which you and the Congress permit them to add to it."[20]

The difference between the Miles idea of protection and the stand-pat variety entertained by the Republican members of the Ways and Means Committee came out crystal-clear in the following colloquy:

MILES: I am a Republican and I want the rate on automobiles to be different . . . the tariff that they have asked for is from two to four times the difference in cost.

Congressman FORDNEY: I am a Republican too and I want the duty made so infernal high that no foreign automobile can get into this country to destroy that labor. That is the difference between two Republicans.[21]

That Miles' own ideas of what constituted a reasonable protective tariff had undergone a change in the course of his campaign for tariff reform was brought out by another Republican member of the Ways and Means Committee, Congressman Dalzell:

MR. DALZELL. I find that you said in the previous May, at the convention of American manufacturers:

"This underlying principle which, in the language of Secretary Taft, requires that each tariff rate shall represent "substantially the permanent differential between the cost of production in foreign countries and that in the United States," is not to be applied in a niggardly way.

---

[20] Hearings, p. 7679.
[21] Hearings, p. 7680.

Enlightened selfishness is a public, as it is a private, virtue. An "ample margin for safety" is as necessary in manufacturing and commercial enterprises as it is in engineering. Full allowance must be made for the contingency of bad times abroad and good times here, for "dumping", for reasonable profits, and for such stability as secures low costs and steady employment. . . .

I am unable to reconcile the statements made by you on several different occasions with respect to that matter. In the issue of American Industries of July 1 last you say: "This 'reasonable profit' clause must not be permitted to become effective. It must be throttled on the edge of the platform, else we never will have an honest, equably adjusted tariff."[22]

Congressman Dalzell was right—Miles had changed his attitude on the subject of protecting profits. In the article to which Dalzell referred, Miles attacked the plank in the Republican platform calling for duties equal to "the difference between the cost of production at home and abroad, together with a reasonable profit to American industries", a plank which was indorsed by Presidential candidate Taft. Miles said the adoption of this principle in tariff making would divide American manufacturers into three classes:

1) Those who are on a sharp competitive basis, 2) those who are more or less loosely joined by "gentlemen's agreements" and 3) the full-fledged trusts and consolidations, of which there are between 200 and 300, in control of most of the great necessities and conveniences of life. . . .

In the fight before us the trusts will, of course, be shrewd enough to put before the subcommittees of Congress the least able in each class. I know a man in the steel business, for instance, whose costs are out of line. He is extremely anxious about the tariff. If rates are made high enough to enable him to make a profit with his out-of-date processes, then in order to keep him going, and a few others who do not total more

[22] Hearings, p. 7648.

than five per cent of the national output, the other 95% will receive at least $40,000,000 more than enough to give them large yearly profits.

The vicious principle of guaranteeing profits places a premium on the easy-going and less active. It is not only vicious—it is un-American.

Every time Miles brought out a striking discrepancy between the cost of production and the excessive duty on a trust-made product, Chairman Payne demanded that he give the source of his information and the name of his informant. Miles spoke of a questionnaire he circulated among his fellow manufacturers 90% of whose replies favored reduction. Chairman Payne wanted to know why they did not come to the hearings. Miles said that some failed to do so for fear of possible unpleasant consequences. Others lacked the initiative and the spirit of sacrifice that would prompt them to absent themselves from their business, incur the expense of a trip to Washington and the loss of time while waiting to be heard.

Miles was particularly shocked by this attitude of the Republican congressmen. Far from putting the burden of proof on those who denied the need of protection, he felt that the burden should be placed on those who demanded protection enabling them to tax the American people. "We want it written over your chairs: 'no proof, no protection'. That would give as good protection as there is on earth."[23]

Finally, as a practical manufacturer familiar with the intricacies of the manufacturing business and cost keeping, he told them bluntly that they lacked the knowledge, the training and the necessary time for ascertaining costs,—a task which should be entrusted to a commission of experts. He wound up that part of his testimony with this plea:

In conclusion, if I may be permitted to say to you what is the desire of 90 per cent of the manufacturers of the United

---

[23] Hearings, p. 7678.

States, in view of the infinite difficulties of the situation and the perplexities of the manufacturing problem, I can only say this: There is a thorough appreciation of the American system of government in all its phases. But the manufacturers of the United States feel that it is absolutely impossible, except upon ceaseless endeavor, either for them or for Congress to discover what are the needs of each and all industries in the way of protection while the consumer is as certain that it is impossible for him or for Congress hastily to determine what are his rights or his privileges in the matter of his purchases and government regulation thereof. Cutlery, earthenware, and pottery—each and all of our various industries—are now operating under a tariff that is extremely inexact, and as Germany and other foreign countries have tariffs that are a thousand times more carefully worked out, it is, in general words, the extreme and insistent desire of those who manufacture and of those who consume that the next tariff be not hastily framed, that it be based upon the absolute truth and the disclosure of all the evidence of the case. It is absolutely clear to such manufacturers and consumers that such disclosures can be made only as the Congress appoint a committee or commission, or whatever it be called—a body of men who will devote themselves absolutely to the problem, will go to the factories, investigate the books of cost, compel the submission of testimony, administer oaths and act upon the principle of a just and fair protection as defined by the President-elect and by the Republican party, through its leaders, and that this body shall, upon the conclusion of its investigations, upon either an early or a remote period, bring back and lay before your honorable committee the full and final data as such a commission only can determine it. Agitation will never cease, the hurt and discomfort of an inaccurate and unfair tariff will never cease, until this commission plan is worked out and made effective. Those who trifle with public opinion and with public patience do it at a very serious risk. This matter has been thought out and worked out with such extreme care and under such compelling circumstances as makes it, in the judgment of all, a necessary step in the solution of the question.[24]

---

[24] Hearings, p. 7665–6.

The strain of his public activity, at the same time that he tried to run a two million dollar business, was making itself felt. On December 29, 1908, three weeks after he concluded his testimony before the Ways and Means Committee, he wrote:

"I am much confused since my return from Washington. I have a big business and I must either almost give up that business to others who in fact ought to manage it or come near quitting my semipublic work.

While I write this I am wanted at a delightful Convention for the advancement of Science at Johns Hopkins Baltimore and last night I had a telegram to come to a town in middle Wisconsin where a Six o'clock Club wants to hear of the Tariff. I am asked to address the Hamilton Club of a thousand members in Chicago this week, and a political economy club in Chicago University. Also invitations for next week and the tariff testimony and one hundred things waiting consideration. Among others a question of a Tariff Commission Convention in Indianapolis."

At the same time his outspoken criticism of the Tariff and the hard blows he delivered at the congressional tariff makers and their big business backers were bound to arouse opposition in the ranks of conservatively minded manufacturers. Writing on January 19, 1909, he said:

"People inside our Association are going after me, as they are after the Ways and Means Committee, and all others probably to try and keep the graft about where it is. I extend something of an olive branch together with a justification for my position in a brief article that will be in January 15th American Industries, and feel pretty sure we will be in shape to hit them another hard rap in a few days. I think stand-patters are a little like a sick patient who has to take his medicine at intervals and not a whole bottleful at once, and I am disposed to give him too big doses and too near together."

Three days later, on January 22, he wrote:

"I am keeping still with some distress and regret and with no end of evidence that I could bring out in answer to criticisms and helpful to my cause. I gave the manufacturers such a shock that it seems necessary to keep quiet for a while. . . .

I have the feeling that things are likely working our way a bit. If they are not I guess I must go ahead with more public statements, take chances on how angry it makes the over-protected interests and how far they can influence rather neutral people against the movement. I do wish I could get a little independent of the over-protected interests."

It was in anticipation of such developments that Miles decided earlier in the year to broaden the base of his support for tariff reform and with the aid of industrialists and business men such as Henry R. Towne, President of Yale & Towne Mfg. Co. and President of the Merchants Association, Alva Johnstone of the Baldwin Locomotive Co., D. M. Parry of Indianapolis, John Kirby of Dayton, O., D. A. Tompkins of Charlotte, N. C., A. H. Sanders, President of the American Reciprocal Tariff League, Nahum I. Batchelder of the National Grange, James S. Agar, President of the American Meat Packers Association, Curtis Guild, Governor of Massachusetts, and several others a conference was held in Washington on February 4, 1908. It was presided over by James W. Van Cleave and resulted in the formation of a Central Committee for the purpose of taking all necessary steps to bring about the realization of the following resolution which was adopted by the conference.

"That for the promotion of the best interests of American industry this conference advocates the immediate creation of a non-partisan permanent tariff commission, for the following purposes and ends, through Congressional action, viz.:

First. The intelligent, thorough and unprejudiced study of facts.

Second. The development and enlargement of our foreign trade.

Third. The accomplishment of this by reciprocal trade agreements, based on maximum and minimum schedules.

Fourth. The adjustment of the tariff schedules so that they shall affect all interests favorably and equitably, without excessive or needless protection to any."

The work of the Committee resolved itself chiefly into speech making and pamphleteering activities by Miles, since it made no provision for paid personnel. Although trained as a manufacturer Miles displayed the journalistic abilities of a born agitator.

The failure of the Republican platform to make any reference to a Tariff Commission, an omission which was likewise conspicuous in Mr. Taft's acceptance speech, and the unconcealed opposition to the idea on the part of the Congressional leaders caused Miles to feel all the more strongly the need of arousing a public demand for the creation of the commission. On his initiative the Central Committee, created in Washington in February 1908, called a national convention which was to meet at Indianapolis February 16–18, 1909.

The February 1, 1909 issue of American Industries opened with an article by President Van Cleave discussing the forthcoming National Tariff Commission Convention at Indianapolis and the proposed permanent Tariff Commission. It quoted President Roosevelt and President-elect Taft in support of a commission. It was followed by articles favoring a permanent Tariff Commission by Senator Beveridge, D. M. Parry, H. E. Miles, and numerous communications from manufacturers' associations, boards of trade, chambers of commerce, farmers' organizations and leaders of public opinion such as President Nicholas Murray Butler of Columbia University and others, and quotations from newspaper editorials all over the country.

With this as a curtain raiser the National Tariff Commission Convention met at Indianapolis on February 16–18, 1909. Its proceedings, together with the speeches made by leaders of business, agriculture and public affairs were reported at length in American Industries of March 1, 1909.[25]

The Convention set up a "General Committee of 100 for a Tariff Commission" representative of the different sections of the country and of the various industrial, agricultural and commercial interests. This Committee elected an Executive Committee of ten members with Mr. Miles as Chairman. In his speech at the Convention reviewing the arguments made against a Tariff Commission, Miles dwelt on the fear expressed by its opponents that

". . . a Tariff Commission will make the tariff a subject of continuous agitation. There is only one reason for continuous Tariff agitation. Every tariff made the old way has been bad in important respects, bad the day it was made and every day thereafter until succeeded by another tariff also bad.

"We are compelled to agitate against error and misuse. Make a tariff right, as Germany did hers and there will be no chance for agitation. We can then make international agreements of twelve years duration as Germany did and agitation will be impossible as well unnecessary and injustifiable."

In his letter of February 19, the day following the adjournment of the Convention, Miles wrote to me:

"Indianapolis Convention was a great success. And its publicity was right good and covered the country. . . . I expect to go to Boston and New York and get those centers organized . . . quickly."

Three days later he wrote from Racine:

"Personally I have stayed in the background for a month or two because of some very vicious assaults made upon me inside our Association and out, . . . but at a meeting of our directors

---

[25] A detailed account of the Convention as well as of the movement for a Tariff Commission was published in 1913 in a 332 page book entitled: "Scientific Tariff Making. A History of the Movement to Create a Tariff Commission" by Henry Tatleton Wills, Secretary of the National Tariff Commission Association.

they passed a vote of a wonderfully considerate resolution in support of my every act as Chairman of the Tariff Committee.

I will be at our headquarters Thursday morning, having been promised by many leaders of organizations in New York that they will organize that city strongly for our movement. One or two of them will go with me to Boston where we have like promises. A delegation will likely also call upon Mr. Taft Friday or Saturday and advise him of the situation. All this furthers our movement better than I had hoped any time recently. It seems to me we will certainly get a Commission within 90 days."

The result of the conference with President-elect Taft was an outspoken declaration by him in favor of a tariff commission.

As Congress opened in special session in March 1909, Mr. Payne introduced his tariff bill. With Miles "lying low" for the time being, President Van Cleave opened the April issue of American Industries with an article bearing the sarcastic title, "The Payne Bill is Argument for a Tariff Commission". The article was summed up in the statement that "the bill fails in its application to the industrial needs of the country and is an irrefutable argument in favor of a Tariff Commission which shall have semi-judicial power to investigate costs".

The campaign bore fruit. When the National Association of Manufacturers assembled for its fourteenth annual meeting in New York on May 17–19, 1909, Miles was able to state in his annual report that

Senator Aldrich, whose distinguished name is given to the present Senate bill, has shown a very kindly interest in the wishes of our Association and has sought to meet them in a substantial way in joining with the other members of his committee, and including in the Aldrich bill, the following provision:

"To secure information to assist the President in the discharge of the duties imposed upon him by Section two of this Act, information which will be useful to Congress in the preparation of tariff legislation and to the officers of the Government in the administration of the customs laws, the President is hereby authorized to employ from time to time, such persons as may be required to make thorough investigations and examinations into the production, commerce and trade of the United States and foreign countries and all conditions affecting the same."

This action of Senator Aldrich which Miles so praised was but a grudging concession to the demand for a full-fledged permanent Tariff Commission demanded by the Manufacturers' Association and provided for in the Beveridge and La Follette bills. Both Senators were strongly opposed to its acceptance, but Miles was reluctant to risk losing this bird in the hand for the larger bird in the bush. Said Miles in his report to the Association:

If this provision becomes a law it is made entirely possible for the President to appoint a tariff body which shall do all those things which our Association deems necessary to the making of future tariffs. The President has so clearly favored a commission, or similar body, that we may reasonably expect that by a reenactment of the Allison proviso, which will be moved by a distinguished Senator, or by the enactment of the Aldrich proviso, we will soon see the tariff put upon that basis of fundamental equity and common sense which will reestablish it in a full measure of popular regard and respect. It is to be noted that the Allison proviso would do this finally and completely; while the Aldrich proviso leaves the accomplishment to executive discretion.

As we shall see, Miles spoke by the book. It was exactly what President Taft did later using a whittled down version of the Aldrich formula as it emerged from the Conference Committee of the two Houses.

In his report Miles drew upon his study of the history of the Tariff Commission idea as it found expression in Congressional enactments over a quarter of a century.

The commission idea is not new; there are thousands of them, local, state and national. Most of the progressive legislation of the past twenty years has been based upon the findings of commissions. Congress appointed a Tariff Commission in 1882. It was given a very brief time in which to do its work. A commission such as we stand for would be much more thorough and helpful. Yet the Commission of 1882 did perform valuable services. The great majority of the rates in the tariff of 1883 are said to have been made upon recommendation of that Commission, while the customs administrative laws and the classifications were as recommended by that Commission and have been little changed to this time.

THE ALLISON COMMISSION PROVISION

A commission is not only constitutional; it is necessary. Our critics should remember that the Senate Finance Committee of 1888, its majority members including Senator Aldrich, Senator Allison and other high protectionists, recommended, as a part of the Allison bill, the creation of a Tariff Commission to be appointed by the President with the advice and consent of the Senate, at salaries of $7,500 each per annum. It gave to that Commission substantially all those powers and duties which our Association desires. It authorized the Commission to look into all sorts of industrial conditions, the effect of particular rates upon "American manufactures and productions," upon "the consumers in respect of causing or contributing to the payment of unreasonable prices," the effect upon agricultural productions, upon "labor and wages in this and other countries." It recognized the principle of international costs in these words:

"To ascertain and compare the actual cost and the selling price, both at wholesale and retail, of similar manufactured commodities . . . in the United States and elsewhere."

Section 48 provided:

"That the Commission shall report its proceedings in respect to the matters hereinbefore mentioned in this act with the statistics and evidence upon which its report is based, together with recommendations for change in customs duties which they may deem advisable and necessary, and the ground upon which its conclusions concerning such changes have been reached, to Congress, in the month of December in each year."

This bill passed the Republican Senate without a dissenting vote from either side of the Chamber, January 22, 1889, and went over to the House, which was then Democratic and engaged upon the Mills Tariff bill. We are informed by some who voted for the Allison bill that, in their judgment, the tariff commission provision would have passed the House and become a law were it not that the session was too far advanced and the members too eager to go home, to give it careful consideration.

A tariff commission, then, in every feature for which our Association stands, is good, constitutional and protectionist doctrine from the standpoint of the party of protection as evidenced by the passage of this bill.

Passing from history to the day's problems Miles called attention to the international aspect of the new tariff.

"A very great responsibility will rest upon the President under the new law in the matter of the application of the maximum and minimum schedules. To impose the new maximum rates upon a foreign nation is to invite a tariff war, those rates being about twenty-five per cent higher than the minimum rates. It cannot be done except after gravest consideration, and it is almost as necessary from a trade standpoint that the minimum rates be not continued except as upon equally careful consideration they are shown to be thoroughly deserved. It is conceded by those best advised that a commission of some sort is necessary in this respect."

We are rather disposed to find the reason for the objection to a tariff commission in the language of a distinguished Senator.

"Those who do not want a tariff commission to find out the facts do not want the facts found out."

Less than a week after the close of the annual meeting, Miles wrote to me on May 25, 1909:

There has been a great fight these last ten days to get me out of the National Association of Manufacturers' tariff work. If out, I would be able to speak much more plainly, and so, help-fully. But others seem to be exposing sufficiently—and I am helpful inside the breastworks as it were. Ten per cent oppos-ing won't control 90% favoring. It will hurt me either way. I am damned for doing, and for not doing. . . . And then the fear of stand-pat criticism—and its lying quality.

I simply served notice last week that I would speak plainly whether liked or not, tho' I'd not attack any particular rates, and I'd go to the public *alone* on that basis rather than put meal in my mouth when I speak.

Speaker Cannon and Chairman of the Ways and Means Com-mittee Payne refused to go even the length of the Aldrich com-promise provision quoted above. As the Act was finally passed it provided in section 2 for the application of maximum and minimum rates of duty to foreign countries and in the concluding sentence of that section made the following provision:

> To secure information to assist the President in the dis-charge of the duties imposed upon him by this section, and the officers of the Government in the administration of the cus-toms laws, the President is hereby authorized to employ such persons as may be required.

However, President Taft in faithful fulfillment of his pre-election promises did what Miles predicted he would do. He gave the broadest interpretation to the Act's grudging authorization and in appointing the first three "such persons" in the fall of 1909 consti-tuted them into a Tariff Board.

During the three years of its existence strenuous efforts were made to get Congress to pass a law creating a Tariff Commission. In January 1911 the National Tariff Commission Association spon-sored a convention which met in Washington. It was attended by some 500 delegates representing industrial, commercial and agricul-tural organizations in 39 states. It was addressed by prominent busi-ness leaders as well as by influential government officials, including

President Taft, leading senators and congressmen of both political parties and both the conservative and "insurgent" legislators of the Republican party, such as Senator Henry Cabot Lodge, Senators Beveridge and Cummings, Congressman Nicholas Longworth and others. The delegates did not content themselves with making speeches and passing resolutions, but made it their business to call on the Senators and Representatives of their respective states to impress upon them the fact that the business community throughout the country was very much in earnest in its demand for a tariff commission.

They left Washington reassured by their representatives in Congress. But the stand-pat group in control of Republican policy in Congress was not ready to relinquish its hold. Although a number of bills were introduced providing for the creation of a Tariff Commission, notably those by Beveridge in the Senate and Longworth in the House, none was enacted. What followed had been foreseen and feared by all advocates of a statutory Tariff Commission: the Sixty Second Congress, which followed, with the House captured by the Democrats, failed to pass an appropriation for the Tariff Board thereby automatically sounding its death-knell. The Board ceased to exist on August 1, 1912.

By one of those odd paradoxes in which American political history abounds, a full-fledged statutory Tariff Commission of the kind Miles and his fellow Republicans had fought for with such zeal, was created four years later by a Democratic Congress at the insistence of President Woodrow Wilson.

Miles, the father of the Tariff Commission, a Republican and protectionist who based his demand for a Commission on the need for accurate determination of the degree of protection required for every product covered by the tariff, lived to see the realization of his ideal by the party he had shunned and which had opposed the idea of a Tariff Commission because it did not believe in a protective tariff.

[67]

II. THE FIGHT AGAINST SPECIAL INTERESTS ON GOVERNMENT BODIES

1. ATTACK ON MAKE-UP OF THE TARIFF COMMISSION

THE TARIFF Board appointed by President Taft in 1909 was composed of Henry C. Emery, Professor of Economics at Yale University, Chairman; Alvin H. Sanders, and James B. Reynolds. All three were Republicans. Emery and Sanders, from their public utterances, were known as moderate protectionists favoring reciprocity agreements. Reynolds was a typical New England hard-boiled protectionist. Later, to meet criticism raised in Congress, President Taft added two Democrats, Professor Thomas W. Page, an economist, and William Howard, a lawyer and former Congressman from Georgia.

Miles had great confidence in the majority of the Board, and in its chief economist, and settled down to await the reports of the Board.

The Board, as previously noted, went out of existence in 1912, after functioning for less than three years. Its published reports on the cotton and woolen textile industries, on the paper and pulp industries, and data on other industries, not ready for publication, were made available to Congress in connection with the Underwood Tariff Bill. It took an active part in negotiations of Reciprocity Agreements, notably with Canada and France.

It was not until 1917 that the law creating the present Tariff Commission was enacted. The Tariff Commission appointed by Woodrow Wilson was made up of men of intellectual attainments and political integrity. It was headed by Frank W. Taussig, Professor of Economics at Harvard University, and outstanding authority on the tariff. Its other two economists, Professor Thomas Walker Page, and William S. Culbertson, had served on the first Tariff

Board. The other three members, David J. Lewis, William Kent, and Edward P. Costigan, were former Congressmen who had the reputation of careful students of the problems they tackled.

Miles regarded the Commission as the embodiment of the ideal he had fought for, and, satisfied that the tariff was at last in the right hands, was content to await results.

With the return of the Republican Party to power after an interval of eight years, the Tariff Commission did not escape the changes of personnel which took place in all departments. A new type of Tariff Commissioner found his way to office under President Harding. The new appointees included Mr. Thomas O. Marvin, former secretary of the Home Market Club of Boston, and lobbyist for high tariff duties on products of New England industries. William Burgess, identified with the pottery industry and for years its lobbyist in Washington, and Henry H. Glassie, son-in-law of former Senator Caffrey of Louisiana, champion of protection for Louisiana's cane sugar.

Miles reacted to the sudden change in Tariff Commission scenery like a bull to a red flag. Once more, fifteen years after he had won the fight for a Tariff Commission, he jumped into the arena. By this time, he had retired from business, and was no longer a member of the National Association of Manufacturers. He felt that the fight for a fair tariff should be based on a broader foundation. The result was the organization of the Fair Tariff League.

2. THE FAIR TARIFF LEAGUE

According to its public announcement, the League consisted "of representatives of 2,500,000 farmers and wage earners, manufacturers, leading women, merchants, and others". Among the organizations represented directly on the General Committee of the League were: the American Farm Bureau Federation, the Farm Bureau Federations of Wisconsin, Minnesota, Vermont, and South Dakota, the

Farmers Unions of Texas, Nebraska, Arkansas, several state Granges, the National Retail Dry Goods Association, the Interstate Cotton Seed Crushers' Association and heads of several corporations engaged in various industries.

The purpose of the League was stated to be

"a just tariff, adequately but not excessively protecting American industry and labor, lowering the cost of living, considerate of our changed position in world affairs . . . (the League) opposes the misuse of protection at the behest of great and selfish interests. It desires cooperation of all who are so minded".

When the Tariff Commission held a hearing on the sugar tariff in January 1924 in which Commissioner Glassie took part, Miles submitted on behalf of the League a fourteen-page brief of which a few extracts follow, in which he fiercely attacked Mr. Glassie and the two other members identified with special interests. Facing these members of the Tariff Commission, he denounced them for sitting in judgment on issues in which they had a personal pecuniary interest:

"Careful consideration of the official record of your Hearings on the Sugar Tariff, January 15, 1924, requires the Fair Tariff League to submit the following brief.

That you are a quasi-judicial body is evidenced by your own statement in the Norwegian Nitrogen Products case wherein you refer to the Commission as exercising 'quasi-judicial power and authority conferred upon it by statute'. . . .

As with every other Court or Commission, you must exemplify the disinterested purity of the Goddess of Justice. Otherwise, there is no reason for your existence, unless an evil one.

What are the facts? Commissioner Glassie has a friendly or family interest of $150,000, par value $200,000, in this sugar investigation. We speak from the records. He has also had for many years, intimate connections with the sugar interests who appear in this case and seek to continue to receive $48,000,000 of additional gross income annually from the present sugar tariff at a cost of $216,000,000 to the American people, which $216,000,000 the sugar tariff is adding to our sugar bill this year.

The part of this $200,000 interest that is closest to him is his wife's ownership of $14,000 of this $200,000 property, being the Columbia Sugar Company, a Louisiana Corporation owning and operating a sugar plantation and mill. So says Mr. Glassie.

The remainder of the property is owned by Commissioner Glassie's four brothers-in-law and one sister-in-law all of whom acquired their interests by inheritance from their father, Senator Caffrey of Louisiana, long the high priest of high protection for Louisiana sugar.

Like Senator Caffrey, probably, whose particular interest in sugar protection is here disclosed, Mr. Glassie insists that his mind cannot be affected by this property interest, and that it is quite different in a husband's mind whether property belongs to his wife or to himself. . . . We need not comment upon a man who insists upon sitting in a case the decision of which is likely to affect the income of his wife and relatives by $20,000 to $30,000 per year, and pleads disinterestedness as his excuse. . . .

But Mr. Glassie goes further. He insists that *nowhere 'has it been held that ownership of stock in a company engaged in an industry which,* as a whole and over the entire country, or over a large section of it, *is affected by a tax or a tariff or any other form of legislation, constitutes in law or in morals an interest in the subject matter of the litigation. . . .' . . .*

And Chairman Marvin, of your Commission in the name of the Commission thanks Mr. Glassie for 'the high sense of public duty which has guided him' in his statement.

Mr. Glassie's participation in this case would not be permitted in any other court or place of adjudication in America or any other first rate country. . . .

Mr. Glassie says that those who differ with him seek 'to establish *a precedent that would forever exclude from the consideration or investigation of an industry affected by a tariff duty, any commissioner * * * having a property interest in the industry,'* or, as Commissioner Costigan says '*a long and intimate relation' with that industry.* Precisely so.

Mr. Glassie's participation in this sugar case, with and because of the approval of his course by Commissioners Marvin and Burgess will definitely establish, by precedent, that each of them and others in due time, may officially determine so far as their power goes, the basis of facts and circumstances upon which duties shall be levied in behalf of industries with which they have been 'long and intimately related,' or perchance have a 'property interest.'

The Chairman of the Commission, Mr. Marvin, makes it a matter of record that a motion was rejected by the Commission, and we know it was by vote of himself, Mr. Glassie and Mr. Burgess—a motion, says Mr. Marvin, declaring and defining, in addition to the statute itself, the qualifications of a member in the respects indicated.

The rule was rejected by vote of Mr. Glassie and two Commissioners who come to this Commission, hot-foot, from the long-time paid service of special interests exceedingly concerned in and profiting by excessive tariff rates. And these Commissioners now refuse to engage not to use their full authority in matters concerning those interests when they come before the Tariff Commission. They support Mr. Glassie in his present position and might as well declare that they will follow his course upon opportunity." . . .

By thus thinking alike and disregarding the rule concerning special interests which other Commissioners and Courts declare to be a requirement of decency, these three men have absolute control of this Commission in this respect, that they can negative any and every attempt, or can limit and consciously or unconsciously misdirect any attempt to apply the 'Flexible' and other provisions of the statutes under which they operate.

They see this. Witness Mr. Glassie's suggestion of what might possibly happen if he withdraws from this case with his family's $150,000 stake in this hearing. Everyone concedes that the remaining five Commissioners would prosecute the case lawfully, but, says Mr. Glassie, 'It is possibly conceivable that three Commissioners constituting a clear majority of five, might have it in their power to affect unfairly and unjustly the recommendations' to the President.

Think of it! A majority of five might 'unfairly and unjustly' affect the conclusions which, says he, 'any one Commissioner,' even himself with his $20,000 interest per annum, could not do.

In fact he stays in this case because he knows that the power of the three men in question is broken if he withdraws and that his vote and theirs have the dominating force above indicated. This is not conjecture. It is the clear record of the past six months.

It is upon this prejudiced and blocked Commission, if we read his message aright, that the President places the initial responsibility of tariff changes under the Flexible Provisions. . . .

What the three together can do is indicated by the Commission's refusal by vote of these three to investigate the Vegetable Oils case, until last week they were ordered to do so by the President. . . .

Doesn't everyone know that Congress requires the Tariff Commission to ascertain costs of production and all other data for use both of the President under the Flexible Provisions, and Congress under its general powers? Doesn't everyone know that Congress appropriated an extra sum of four hundred thousand dollars in September 1922, seventeen months ago, for the immediate and continuous use of the Commission in investigating the fairness and desirability of the rates of duty enacted September 21, 1922? . . .

Congress said investigate. You didn't.

Doesn't everyone know that when you did begin investigations six months later that instead of considering the vital items, steel, textiles, chinaware, glass, aluminum, and the four trusts then under indictment of the Federal Courts for 'arbitrary and excessive' price fixing—instead of investigating these and other great aggregations whose tariff rates cost the public annually one or two billion dollars, you began to investigate—what? Wooden handles for paint brushes, a chemical used in a gargle, wall pockets, artificial flowers, and, not the file trust, but Swiss files, tiny things used by jewelers and not made here in any quantity; not the plate glass trust, but only plate glass used for mirrors; not the over-protected hosiery industry, but only cotton hosiery for infants; and in short a list of seventeen products of almost no concern to the public, except sugar which we here discuss, and casein, a product of milk.

Doesn't everyone know that this action was against the will of the people's Commissioners known for ten years to be utterly without selfish interests, and upon the insistence of others?

Information from all sections of the country indicates a loss of public confidence in the Commission. Confidence is a delicate thing. It can be retained only by an observance of the delicacies of every situation.

Mr. Glassie couldn't sit on a petit jury to determine damages if his wife's auto had run over a chicken. . . .

As Mr. Glassie says, his course establishes a precedent. If Mr. Burgess follows it, and the records assure us that he will, then his vote on the pottery schedule will be that of a man who for many years was the paid representative in Washington and elsewhere for some of the greatest of those interests, and during these years exercised for them a zeal in the procurement of the highest obtainable tariff rates on their goods that necessarily has shaped his mind beyond possibility of present entirely judicial consideration.

As a single instance, he did all in his power to have the importation of certain French chinaware advanced in value in the Customs House. He did not leave the matter to the judgment of the Customs House officials of the United States. He was in France together with special Treasury agents which latter, it appeared, he dominated, and brought back a lot of evidence which, when submitted on reappraisement and reappraisement cases to the General Appraiser, was by the latter in his official report pronounced as *'discredited'* which words, lawyers tell us, mean in common speech discreditable.

The fact that the judge in that case *discredited* his evidence indicates without any other illustration, of which there are many, how likely it may be that when he would determine the action of this semi-judicial and supposedly impartial tariff tribunal in respect to the pottery interests he could not do it safely and would be liable again to have set against his action the word 'discredited.' Why should the public suffer from even the suspicion of such a possibility? The public wants its Commissioners to be, like Caesar's wife, above suspicion.

If Mr. Burgess is to exercise authority when the pottery cases come up, the public, or a great part thereof, will feel forced to believe that sugar has its vote on this Commission, Pottery has its, Textiles its, and will wonder when Steel, Plate Glass, and Aluminum will have theirs, to determine by what right the latter so-called trusts are adding all of their duties plus freights on competing imports from Europe, and more, to their domestic prices, when they are known to produce more cheaply, or substantially as cheaply as any competitors in the world. The people will wonder whether tariff-fattened trusts now under indictment in federal Courts and others recently sent to jail for 'arbitrary and excessive' price-fixing are to be investigated, and what use anyway is this sort of tribunal. The public will feel helpless—a bad situation.

If Commissioner Marvin is to vote in respect to the interests that he has served with utter zeal for so many years, what shred of reputation will be left in this fact-finding, so-called impartial, semi-judicial, non-partisan tariff commission?

The Home Market Club of Boston that Mr. Marvin served as Secretary and General Manager, if we may use the latter terms, is one of the principal agencies of certain New England manufacturers, mostly of cottons, woollens, and silks, commonly known to have grossly exploited the tariff by the help of the Home Market Club. The Tariff Commission itself in various of its findings, and the records of Congress, support this statement that their tariff rates are excessive.

The Home Market Club is commonly believed, we might say known, to have perverted public sentiment and public knowledge for tens of years. It opposed the creation of this semi-judicial, fact-finding body, and this in the confident belief of thousands or tens of thousands of informed Americans, because it didn't want the facts found out. Its members are high-class men, but extremely partisan. They pursue this unhappy course because to many of them, as we will shortly prove, the tariff is like poker, a game of bluff and cunning, with a code quite different from ordinary morals; or, in other cases, and there are many, their zeal is identical with that exhibited by Mr. Burgess in the Pottery Case cited. . . .

In conclusion, there essentially is no reason on earth for the existence of this Commission except that it be impartial and disinterested. All else follows and depends on that. It is this character of disinterestedness and therefore of trustworthiness that is now being destroyed."

Miles' attack, coupled with the fact that three of the commissioners who had been appointed by President Wilson—Costigan, Lewis, and Culbertson—had also challenged Glassie's right to sit on the sugar case, bore fruit. Congress tacked on a "rider" to the Tariff Commission appropriation bill, providing that no member of the Commission could draw a salary who sat on a case in which he was interested.

With Glassie thus eliminated, the Commission by a vote of three to two voted to recommend to the President a reduction of the duty on sugar by one-half cent per pound. But President Coolidge took no action on the recommendation, thus lending his silent support to the ex-lobbyist minority. Soon after he eliminated from the Commission the three holdovers from the Wilson administration.

3. ATTACK ON SPECIAL INTERESTS ON CONGRESSIONAL COMMITTEES

Miles did not hesitate to carry his fight against special interests in Government to higher levels than the Tariff Commission.

When the Committee on Agriculture of the House of Representatives appointed a special subcommittee in 1937 to deal with the subject of sugar, Miles attacked it on the same grounds as he had the appointees of President Harding thirteen years before. In the course of his testimony before the subcommittee on March 22, 1937, the following colloquy took place:

"MR. MILES: Now, I must say a word about the committee. I am going to hold you gentlemen in happy remembrance all my life. You are about as good as you know how to be. Now it is not your fault that you do not know how. The trouble is you are too American in using its evil practices in legislation. The chairman of this committee, whom, as I say, I love and honor, could not sit on a jury trying a dog case, if he were interested in the dog. He is a big sugar grower, and was paid, until he came to Congress, for representing the sugar interests of the United States for a great . . .

MR. CUMMINGS: Yes; $3 a day, when I worked for them.

[76]

MR. MILES: Well, while we are talking about it, tell us what Mr. Kennedy gets?

MR. CUMMINGS: No; I do not know the gentleman.

MR. MILES: Mr. Kearney, I mean. They always get very attractive men as lobbyists, you know. Mr. Kearney is a delightful, intelligent gentleman. He is not giving his time for nothing down here representing those who want to get more of other people's money, more and more, and when they are getting $410,000,000, they want to make it $510,000,000 for a crop that can be bought for $34,500,000 at our ports.

MR. CUMMINGS: Let us be fair.

MR. MILES: Yes.

MR. CUMMINGS: This committee is supposed to know a bit about sugar.

MR. MILES: How is that?

MR. CUMMINGS: We are on this Committee because we are supposed to know a bit about sugar.

MR. MILES: Just a bit; yes sir.

MR. CUMMINGS: I do not want to get it too high. I did not want to put it up too high.

MR. MILES: No; I would hate to do that. I really could not do that.

MR. CUMMINGS: Just about that much (indicating part of a finger's length).

MR. MILES: Well, thereabouts.

MR. CUMMINGS: Now, I admit that you thoroughly understand the tariff. . . . You are objecting to us because we thought we did know a little bit about sugar.

MR. MILES: You are interested parties, every one of you is colored with interest, deeply colored."

This colloquy was supplemented by a published statement signed by Miles as Chairman of the Fair Tariff League, from which the following is an extract:

"ANOTHER SUGAR TAX OF $100,000,000"

"Another Congressional Committee 'Packed' by Profiteers"

"For fifty years in Tariff making and otherwise, Congress has delegated the proposals of profiteering groups to formal or informal subcommittees picked to please the profiteers.

[77]

The chairmanship of the subcommittees to determine duties, subsidies, etc. for sugar went as a sort of right or perquisite to Congressman Timberlake, from our greatest sugar-producing area in Northern Colorado.

When Timberlake was succeeded by Congressman Cummings, a big sugar grower, the latter naturally succeeded to this chairmanship. Upon his election to Congress, he resigned his position as the official leader of the sugar growers because, as another leader and associate said, 'It wouldn't look well for a Congressman to be the official agent of sugar growers and sugar mills.'

The other members of the sub-committee were hand-picked from sugar-growing states east of the Rockies whose people pay $77,000,000 annually in taxes to 'protect' their crops that could be bought for less than $2,000,000, from over-seas, delivered at our sea-ports; and including in addition Michigan and Ohio whose people pay $38,000,000 in sugar subsidies to get $6,000,000 of sugar grown in their states. Also upon the Committee was the Representative from Hawaii to assure the continuation of its sugar subsidies of over $52,000,000 which equals $150 for every adult and baby there, or $750 per family. Likewise, Porto Rico's Representative to continue its subsidies of about $44,600,000.

What a bunch to decide what our consumers shall pay, with the present subsidies costing them $410,000,000 annually to get $34,500,000 of sugar grown in the states, international values above.[26]

As the Interior Department said last month (May bulletin, Volume 27, Number 5) 'without exception every recommendation of the administration with respect to the division of quotas was disregarded in favor of a set of provisions believed to have been proposed in large part by the cane refiners.

The subcommittee bill has met the strong opposition of the Departments of Agriculture, State and Interior because it would constitute what is considered to be an indefensible destruction of export trade.' There has resulted a deadlock in the House Committee which will not yield to the judgment of the administration nor to the rights of the public.

---

[26] By "international values" Miles meant the value in overseas markets where the sugar originated.

III. THE THIRTEEN YEAR WAR ON THE
SUGAR TARIFF

1. A CHALLENGING RE-DEFINITION OF TARIFF PROTECTION

MILES FOLLOWED up his first attack on the personnel of the Tariff
Commission with a brief on the Sugar Tariff which he submitted
to the Tariff Commission seven weeks later on April 10, 1924. The
permanent value of that brief lies not so much in the devastating
criticism of the sugar tariff, as in the further contribution which
Miles made in applying the principle of difference in cost of production at home and abroad as a measure of protection, which had
been officially accepted by the Republican Party sixteen years earlier
on Miles' initiative.

Citing a Congressional investigation of the paper-making industry, in 1907–08, which found that

"The difference in the cost of production between up-to-
date, well-located plants and inefficient, badly-located plants
in this country, was greater than the difference between efficient
plants here and efficient plants abroad,"

Miles raised this question:

"Should we have excessive rates to protect the inefficient, or
low rates for the efficient? The rule does not say. . . ."

This question had plagued the economists of the Tariff Board
and the Tariff Commission for years, but it remained for Miles,
the business man and champion of "an honest tariff" to challenge
the traditional concept of tariff protection.

To show how serious this question is, Miles proceeded to analyze the situation in the sugar industry. He pointed out that the

"Eastern seaboard factories that refine imported raw (cane) sugar make a net profit of half a cent per pound."[27] On the other hand, "The Great Western makes nearer three cents per pound, while its (beet) growers all but starve at the minimum contract price of $5.50 per ton. The Great Western Sugar Company . . . is a consolidation of other factories (existing) in 1905. It began with paid-in preferred stock of $15,000,000 and common stock of $10,544,000: all water. It is an over-powering influence in the beet sugar situation and typical of its competitors.

For the seven years ending February 28, 1923, the Great Western Sugar Company's net earnings after all charges and preferred dividends, averaged $12 on its watered common stock of $25 par value. . . . The President of this company says: 'Since organization in 1905, the Company had disbursed as dividends on its common stock (once all water) $36,308,177 in cash and $4,428,500 in common stock, and after paying such dividends has a surplus exceeding $30,000,000."

Miles proceeded to drive home his new question:

"The point is that we have a rule for the application of the protective principle, but no definition of protection itself, and its limitations.

Are we to protect ignorance, shiftlessness, incapacity, plants that are out of date? . . . Are we to protect plants that are so badly located or so badly managed, that the same conditions in a non-protected industry would put them out of business?

If we are to do this, then protection becomes an alms-house and asylum for cripples and incompetents, and all such must be protectionists, demanding profits and good living by tariff legislation. . . .

In fact, protection, honestly considered, can be given only to those industries and persons that are efficient, especially

[27] In this Miles erred, since half a cent represented the gross margin.

[80]

adapted in equipment, location, efficiency and circumstances assuring successful production at as low cost to the consuming public as prevails in non-protected occupations, where the most capable make large profits and the unfortunate have to quit.

That is: Protection requires the use of every ordinary advantage in the way of training and efficient personal capacity, favorable natural conditions and adequate equipment.

It is not for the growing of bananas in Florida, nor the maintenance at public expense through the tariff of the slothful, the inefficient or the unfortunate.

Furthermore, at any protective rate, were it double present rate, people will enter the protected industry under less and less advantageous circumstances and a considerable percentage of these will be unfortunate and cry for more.

For these reasons and in the belief that we are only formulating a universally accepted, but not hitherto definitely expressed, judgment of Congress and the public, we would extend the accepted principle of differences in costs as follows:

Under this rule of 'the difference in costs here and abroad' are to be considered only such domestic interests as produce under conditions thoroughly favorable as respects management, equipment, location and markets, and, in agriculture, under favorable soil conditions and climate.

With protection thus understood, the rule of the difference in costs is of extreme value, although it cannot be applied as easily and expeditiously as a yard-stick to a piece of cloth."

While economists have repeatedly pointed out that the protective tariff protects inefficient plants and by so doing retards industrial progress, Miles was the first business man to draw the obvious conclusion from that fact, and refined the formula of "difference in costs at home and abroad" by excluding production costs of obsolete, inefficient plants. Although over a quarter of a century has elapsed since Miles thus reformulated the principle of protection, it still awaits official recognition by the party of protection.

[81]

2. FRONTAL ATTACK ON THE SUGAR TARIFF

Once having gotten his teeth into the sugar tariff, Miles would not let go, and with bull-dog tenacity, kept up his fight until almost the end of his life. After submitting his 1924 brief to the Tariff Commission, he kept reverting to the subject for the next thirteen years. Whenever the subject of sugar came up before a Congressional Committee, Miles was sure to make his appearance and hammer away at the gross iniquity of the sugar tariff.

In March, 1934, the Fair Tariff League published a thirty-six page pamphlet summarizing the various statements on sugar which Miles had made in the preceding decade. On June 14, 1936, he appeared before the Senate Committee on Finance to attack the bill for a proposed processing tax on sugar to be levied in addition to the import duty. On March 22, 1937, he appeared before a Special Subcommittee of the House Committee on Agriculture.*

Miles' intensive study of the sugar industry over a period of some fifteen years, finally led him to the conclusion that there was absolutely no justification for any duty on sugar. Pointing out that sugar cane was a tropical product, he proceeded to prove that its cultivation in Louisiana was on a par with trying to raise bananas and pineapples in hot-houses under tariff protection.

As for the sugar beets from which Western refineries were producing beet sugar, he contrasted their insignificance in the total sugar output with the fantastic cost to the country of trying to foster that industry. While the beet sugar refiners were the prime movers and beneficiaries of a duty on raw sugar, their ostensible justification of the duty lay in the protection of the farmers raising sugar beets.

Miles branded this as a hollow pretense and contrasted the enormous tax paid by the American consumers of sugar with the insig-

---

* See pp. 76–78.

nificant value of the domestic (raw) sugar output. While the tax in the two preceding years (1935–1936) imposed an additional burden on the consumer equal to $410,000,000 per annum, the value of the domestic crop in 1935 at the world price (i.e. without duty) was only $34,500,000; in other words, the tax was 12 times the value of the crop raised.[28]

Using official statistics, Miles showed that out of 6,288,648 farms in the United States, only 42,000 farms or only a fraction of one per cent of all farmers, raised sugar beets or cane. Taking the total acreage under cultivation in the United States, he showed that for every 100 acres under cultivation, there was only one third of an acre under sugar.

Going a step further, Miles obtained an estimate of the value of all the lands in the United States devoted to the cultivation of sugar beets and sugar cane. This covered the states of California, Colorado, Idaho, Louisiana, Michigan, Montana, Nebraska, Ohio, Utah, Washington, Wyoming and five other states with small acreages. The estimates by the experts of the Farm Loan Board placed the value of all these lands in 1932 (which had not changed materially at the end of 1936) at $78,287,000.

Miles thus summed up the situation in business vernacular:

"You can buy all the sugar land in the United States with four months of the sugar tax. You can buy it and give it to the birds and save the people $400,000,000 a year thereafter. You can buy all the factories that refine home-grown sugar with another three or four months of the sugar taxes and give them to the bats.

In fact, the book value of the mills (far greater than the real value) has been paid in sugar taxes by a hoodwinked

---

[28] In this figure Miles frankly disregarded the value of the sugar raised in our dependencies—Puerto Rico, Hawaii and the Philippines—which were also beneficiaries of the U. S. tariff on sugar.

public sixty times over, with this fact kept from them by uninformed or prejudiced Congressmen and others, who let the public think that these taxes are for the growers only or almost entirely, when it is from one half of these taxes that the sugar mills make their so-called profits, if any. They are wholly parasitic. They don't make a penny from mill operations. They even lose a large part of their parasitic bounties, of which fact the public is ignorant.

To encourage the raising of each $1 worth of sugar, international value, in the United States, we paid in 1935 and 1936 that dollar and about $12 additional to get it grown in the United States.

I wonder how many of you realize that in 1935 and again in 1936 we paid $410,000,000 of sugar taxes to get $34,500,000 of sugar at world prices grown in the United States each of these years?"

Of the $410,000,000 which Miles estimated the sugar duty cost the American consumer annually, the government collected only forty million dollars in duties. The rest represented the pyramiding of mark-ups and profits on the duty paid as the sugar passed from the growers, to the refiner, the wholesaler, the retailer, and through similar stages on products containing sugar, such as candy, pastries, preserves, jellies, etc.

Taking up the financial reports of the six leading companies refining domestic sugar: the Great Western, the Michigan Sugar Co., American Crystal, Amalgamated, Utah and Idaho Companies, and Holly Sugar Company, Miles showed that their combined net book profit from the 1935 crop amounted to $12,315,000 while their "monopoly income" that is the excess charges to the consumer which they were enabled to make with the aid of the Government tax was equal to $28,203,000. In other words, but for the tariff and processing taxes, they would have shown a loss of nearly sixteen million dollars.

Miles pointed out that

"the financial record of the mills has been deplorable as a whole, for many years, in good times and bad. No consumer-tax possible will enable these very costly mills to make a profit with only 80 per cent running from sixty to seventy days per year. They are overbuilt 100 per cent. In Louisiana there are 60 mills, many of them badly located, where 20 would suffice, if well located."

He concluded this part of his analysis of the domestic sugar industry with these pointed remarks:

"This is not said with ill will, but because honesty requires consideration of the facts.

If the mills had been closed and the Federal Treasury had sent them their proclaimed 'profits', the public debt would have been less by $16,000,000 per annum.

Just as the annual sugar taxes were five times the value of the acreage in sugar in 1932, so the tax is three times the book value of the mills, and nearly five times the value of their used capacity. And the sugar taxes paid since 1897 is 60 times their book value, or 87 times the value of the capacity used in 1932.

By rights shouldn't the title to these mills now rest in the public?"

Striking as these figures were, Miles did not stop there. The most astonishing consequence of the sugar duty proved to be the damage it had inflicted on the agricultural economy of the United States.

At the height of the period of intensive trade with Cuba, which coincided with the first World War and the years immediately following, when Cuban sugar was in great demand, exports from Cuba reached the record figure of $794,000,000 in 1920, of which the United States took 627 million dollars' worth. This great volume of exports enabled Cuba to buy abroad on a generous scale, her total imports during that year amounting to 557 million dollars, of which the United States furnished over 404 million dollars' worth.

To present a conservative estimate of the damage caused by our duty on raw sugar, Miles took as his base the year 1928, by which time our exports to Cuba had dropped to the comparatively modest sum of $129,000,000. At that time the duty on Cuban sugar under the Fordney-McCumber Tariff amounted to 1.76 cents per pound. In 1930, the Hawley-Smoot Tariff raised the duty on Cuban sugar still higher: to two cents a pound. This marked the culmination of a process of steadily advancing rates with each Republican revision of the Tariff from the time that the McKinley Act of 1890 had placed raw sugar on the free list.

To go back to Miles' basic year of 1928, our imports from Cuba amounted to 203 million dollars. They went up to 209 million the following year, only to register a precipitous drop to 116 million in 1930, when the Hawley-Smoot Act imposed a two cent duty on Cuban sugar. Sugar imports declined further in the ensuing years, with corresponding declines of our exports to Cuba as shown by the following figures:

Year	U. S. Imports From Cuba millions of dollars	U. S. Exports to Cuba millions of dollars
1928	203	129
1929	209	127
1930	116	92
1931	89	46
1932	81	28
1933	84	23
1934	108	41
1936	102	56
1936	122	66

The drop in our exports to Cuba affected all our agricultural exports, including cattle, hogs, meat, and dairy products, eggs, grains, fruits, vegetables and vegetable oils.

Instead of following the usual form of presentation by citing the figures of exports of these products, Miles resorted to a more striking comparison in terms of acres of land rendered idle through the falling off of our exports. With the aid of experts of the Department of Agriculture, the estimate arrived at was 954,000 acres, which drew this comment from Herbert Miles:

"Now, as to the abandonment of 954,000 acres of plowed land because of our present sugar policy, Cuba, in the peak of crazy times, bought half a billion dollars in a year, but the following comparison is for 1928 when her purchases were conservative, only $125,000,000.

In 1933 Cuba used 954,000 less of our tilled acres than in the year 1928, because in 1933 she could not pay for the products of that 954,000 acres in sugar because we would not let her. Consequently, Cuba had not less than 2,000,000 acres of idle sugar land, and many of her sugar and other laborers starved to death for want of work. We had here millions of acres of rich, idle, plowed land, unused because we could not sell the surplus crops that they would produce. We were paying farmers $10 an acre for keeping the land idle, and we are keeping great numbers of farm laborers on relief rolls."[29]

After citing experts' figures showing how much more profitable the cultivation of the sugar beet acres could be made by raising alfalfa, potatoes, barley, cabbage, beans, dairy products, poultry and eggs, Miles closed the subject of the Tariff on sugar with this striking presentation of the folly of protection run mad:

"Protection to American industries is not madness. It is based on common sense. The great farm leader who says American farmers want free sugar is like McKinley, Cannon, Aldrich, and a Committee of Nebraskans (Mr. Kearney's state) farmers, one of whom said, 'Better keep these sugar growers in the poor house than endure this tax.' These people want free sugar like free bananas, because, as President Hoover said,

---

[29] Hearings, House Committee on Agriculture, March 22, 1937, p. 19.

'Sugar cannot be grown in the United States," meaning not reasonably grown.

Contrast our mills operating variously from 61 to 70 days per year with Cuba's running 5 to 8 months per year, and easily 8 months if we will exchange our foodstuffs for Cuban sugar.

This exchange would give us (to the extent of the exchange) sugar absolutely without cost, free as water in this sense that we would pay for it with acres now plowed under and kept idle at a rental charge of $10 per acre paid by the Federal Government.

The gain would be the same to Cuba, except greater, because sugar is her main dependence. In both countries thousands of workers would be taken off relief rolls with their self-respect restored."[30]

---

[30] Hearings, p. 25.

IV. CRIME, PINEAPPLES AND THE TARIFF
COMMISSION

UNDER THIS title Miles published through the Fair Tariff League a
scathing attack on the incredible tariff on pineapples. It was spread
on the pages of the Congressional Record by Senator Walsh of
Montana on August 4, 1932.

It was an attack in the best Miles style not only on the absurdity
of levying a duty on a tropical fruit which could not be profitably
raised in the United States, but on the depth of evasiveness, cow-
ardice and disingenuousness to which, the Tariff Commission, as then
constituted, had sunk. A part of the statement is reproduced below.

> The report of the Tariff Commission on pineapples is just
> from the press.
>
> In its statement of "findings and conclusions" to the Presi-
> dent the commission represents only one table of cost com-
> parisons, giving the difference in costs of Florida and Cuban
> pineapples delivered in New York City and Chicago.
>
> The table is false because no Florida pineapples are shipped
> to either place. None in the last four years excepting eight
> carloads to New York in 1928 and six carloads to Chicago in
> 1929.
>
> Imports can not compete with the Florida product except in
> Florida, where its entire product is consumed, or "just van-
> ishes," as an informed expert says, sold by the roadside and
> in not-distant villages and cities, as apples were sold 50 years
> ago before the industry was standardized in production and
> marketing, and each producer delivered his small stock for
> consumption near by.
>
> Out of 6,000,000 American farmers, and 59,000 in Florida,
> only 11 farmers, and those in Florida, grew pinapples last
> year and on 86 acres. They produced less than 5,000 crates,

worth $10,000. Their fields are neglected. In good practice, as in Cuba, fields are replanted by the third year. In Florida 29 per cent of the plantings are 11 years old, 52 per cent are from 8 to 11 years old, and only 15 per cent are 4 years or less. The fields are just too good to plow up and 59,000 Florida farmers are too wise to plant pineapples. Cuba's production is about 40 per cent per acre greater than Florida's, per the commission's report.

The industry was considered prosperous when there was no foreign competition of consequence and Cuba and Porto Rico were starving untaught, neglected, and wretched folk in jungles under Spanish misrule.

Nor are pineapples an infant industry. They have been grown in Florida for 72 years, since 1860, and the 11 farmers and 86 acres are all that are left of it. There were 13 farmers and 88.5 acres in 1930 when Congress increased the tariff 42 per cent to keep them going, but two of them knew better and quit.

The value of the crop in 1930 was $15,000, and in 1931, $10,000. If the growers got full benefit of the tariff, then 13 farmers in 1930 got a tariff bonus of $2,996, or $230 each; and in 1931, 11 farmers got a tariff bonus of $1,980, or $180 each.

In order that they might get this instead of raising other Florida crops of which the Nation never gets enough, the public was taxed at the customs houses about $563,000 in 1930, with $448,000 of this sum paid on imports that were consumed before June when the Florida crop ripened.

As pineapples, landed in New York, duty paid, were worth 8 cents each and retailed at 30 to 60 cents, with the prices varying greatly according to the market, it is reasonable to suppose that the duty was trebled in retail prices and cost consumers $1,500,000. It certainly cost much more than one million per year. This to keep 11 farmers from plowing up 86 acres that could be as well used otherwise, as 59,000 other farmers in Florida knew.

All these facts were given the commissioners by their able agricultural division and are discoverable, not in the letter to the President but in dry statistical tables, largely disassociated and serviceable only upon diligent analysis and rearrangement, confirmed and assured by the help of experts.

Why didn't the commission tell the President the truth directly and clearly? In the recent debate in the Senate on the Tariff Commission, Senator Smoot and others emphasized that it is mandatory upon the commission to disclose every important fact.

The commission did tell the President that the two years, 1930 and 1931, upon which its costs of production were figured, suffered from a frost in March, 1930, and cold weather during the growing season in 1931, and that these years were "not normal." In the summary, however, the commission said, "No data are available showing a normal year." In fact it is the good year, if any, that is abnormal. As the commission told the President, since 1910, 22 years ago, there have been crop shortages, loss of vigor, decreasing yields, heavy freezes and abandonment of acreage. Also, "the chief cause of the decline of the pineapple industry in Florida is red wilt, a fungus disease traceable to the soil, causing the roots to rot."

Consequently, the 1909 acreage of 3,527 was reduced to 229 acres in 1919, 125 acres in 1929, and 86 acres in 1931, after the tariff grabbers had hoped to better conditions by increasing the tariff 42 per cent the year before.

The commission knew all this and more, as hereafter disclosed.

It dodged the issue and tried to dodge all responsibility by stating its position, in three lines only, as follows: "After consideration of the facts (only a few of which were given the President in their statement to him) obtained in this investigation the commission does not specify an increase or a decrease in the duties on fresh pineapples". . . .

In a sense, pineapples are trifling; but it is not a trifle to find that a commission, vested particularly with the public interest, hasn't stamina enough to face a trifle. It seeks to save its skin by putting the facts in an accompanying general summary, decipherable only upon greater labor than a hired servant, the commission can, in decency, require or expect.

We have done our utmost to ruin Cuba by unwise tariff exactions. She has retaliated again and again purely for self-defense. She can not admit imports from us that she can not pay for. She produces approximately 700,000 crates on nearly 6,000 acres. She sends to New York and Chicago, 1,200 to 1,700 carloads annually. Why not surprise her with a friendly gesture; make the pineapple duty only nominal; double her production; break down our retailers' price monopoly by means of an abundant supply; and let millions of us eat pineapple? Let Cuba prosper in one industry, at least.

V. THE FORDNEY-McCUMBER TARIFF

THE reader will recall the colloquy which occurred between Miles and Congressman Fordney of Michigan when Miles was testifying before the Ways and Means Committee on the Payne-Aldrich tariff bill in 1908.[31]

Thirteen years had passed since and by virtue of the seniority rule which governs the promotion of members of Congress on Congressional Committees Mr. Fordney rose to the chairmanship of the all powerful Committee on Ways and Means.

His advancement to the chairmanship coincided with the recapture of Congress by the Republican Party after eight years of Democratic control under the Wilson administration. The revision of the Underwood (Democratic) tariff was, therefore, in order and the extreme protectionist views of the new chairman of the Committee on Ways and Means forecast an orgy of prohibitive duties.

Miles had not forgotten Fordney's conception of Protection and took it as a threat to the principle of basing protection on the difference between the costs of production at home and abroad which he had been instrumental in getting the Republican Party to adopt thirteen years earlier. He knew it would be a waste of effort to argue with Fordney and held his fire until the bill reached the Senate.

In opening his testimony before the Senate Committee on Finance, Miles said:

> The Fair Tariff League is composed wholly of protectionists, manufacturers, representatives of 2,500,000 farmers and wage earners, women's associations, merchants and others. . . .

---

[31] See p. 54.

We are thoroughly opposed to excessive rates, knowing them to be tremendously injurious to the national interests. We find many industries operating under excessive tariff rates th.t are no more "protection" than burglary is honest work.[32]

And then he proceeded with a wealth of illustrations filling sixty closely printed pages of the Hearings to make good his charge of "tariff burglary." Displaying a pair of socks which he had bought at a "five and ten" store for ten cents, he said:

The cheap socks I show you are one of the miracles illustrating our accomplishment. Our hosiery used to come from France and Germany. To-day there are shop windows in Chemnitz, the German hosiery center, displaying American hose, while our silk hosiery is freely sold in the stores of Paris.

Thirty years ago a single operator ran six of the machines of those days, making a total of 18 dozen pairs of socks daily, with a piece-rate wage of 3 cents per dozen pairs, giving her 54 cents per day.

Twenty years ago, with better machines and the same rate per day, the output was double, giving her a wage of $1.08 per day.

In the last five years, with full automatic machines making the entire sock including the ribbed top, each operator runs 25 machines, knitting 150 dozen pairs daily. Her piece rate has been reduced from 3 cents to 2 cents per dozen pairs, and yet she makes $3 per day.

These socks cost 81.6 cents per dozen pairs today, including 36 cents for the yarn. They retail at 10 cents per pair in the 10 cent stores. . . . This is the miracle and perfect accomplishment of protection. Two cents per dozen pairs for knitting on the piece basis and $3 per day wage. The total labor cost from raw cotton to finished sock is 2 cents per pair; the lowest wage cost in the world and the highest weekly earnings paid any hosiery people in the world.

A single operator runs from 20 to 30 of the newest type machines knitting women's silk hose and producing a total of 80 to 90 dozen pairs daily. At 4 cents per dozen pairs, or one-third of 1 cent per pair, she would earn $3 per day. . . .

[32] Hearings before the Committee on Finance, U. S. Senate, on the Proposed Tariff Act of 1921. (Volume 5) Appendix, p. 5359.

Contrast these facts with the tariff attitude of the hosiery and knit-goods people. One of their typical representatives declares that they can not exist without a further increase in their tariff, because says he, average wages in the United States in this industry are $30 per week, in England $17.40 per week, in Germany $5.50, in France $7.14. Were he to tell the truth, he would say that the wage cost per dozen pairs in the United States is about 2 cents per pair on socks and twice that on women's silk hose of ordinary quality, and correspondingly more for "full fashioned" . . . nor does any country pay less than he does per pair. That is why one-fourth of all the hosiery and knit goods made in the United States is exported the world over; that is why we exported hosiery last year to the amount of $4,000,000 and imported only $1,000,000, the imports being mostly novelties, golf stockings, etc. that we did not care to make. . . .

Notwithstanding this, the House bill with its American valuation clause puts higher duties on cotton, wool and artificial silk hosiery than are given laces, which have always been thought to carry the highest rates in our tariffs. This is done by compound duties that hide the robbery. . . .

With Congress virtually prohibiting importations by a high tariff in this, as in other industries, and our domestic manufacturers with their heads together on prices, the people are paying unreasonably for their supplies. Mercerized children's socks, that were from 85 to 90 cents per dozen before the war, are now $2.50. Fortunes have been made in the hosiery business in the last few years. . . . It is for Congress and the people to say whether these manufacturers shall henceforth be self-supporting or shall longer have great and unnecessary grants of public funds.

The story of hosiery is repeated in almost every other industry.[33]

And Miles proceeded with specific proofs for the rest of his sixty-page testimony of which his hosiery story is typical.

"The world is short of sugar and yet Cuba, with enormous supplies, is searching desperately for buyers,"[34] said Miles and pro-

[33] Hearings, pp. 5361–62.
[34] Hearings, p. 5384.

ceeded to enlighten the Senate Committee with information which the reader will find in our chapter on sugar.

He cited similarly striking facts on glass and glassware, plate-glass, steel files, aluminum and aluminum-ware, oilcloth and linoleum, asbestos, furs, clocks, carpets and rugs, toys and games, steel and steel products, lead, tin, tinware. Speaking of the latter Miles with dry humor volunteered this piece of gossip: "The McKinley and Payne duties on tin plate and tinware were admirable in conception but excessive in amount. They resulted in the marriage of an exceedingly rich American widow to a royal prince, and a charming princess to an American youth. We have several princesses now; we want cheap tinware."[35]

He continued his recital of figures—on automobiles for which the makers asked a 30 per cent duty and congress "thrust upon the industry not less than 45 per cent" under American valuation; on musical instruments, umbrellas, hardware, bolts and nuts, manufactures of brass, bronze and copper and many other products.

One of the features of the Fordney bill which aroused Miles' indignation was the new administrative provision that ad valorem "duties shall be levied upon the basis of domestic wholesale prices" instead of the wholesale price of the commodity in its country of origin.

Since the definition of protection implied the equalization of foreign and domestic costs through a tariff duty equal to the difference between them, the ad valorem duty was always based on the foreign cost. To base it on the domestic price meant to base the duty not on the difference in cost, but on whatever price the American manufacturer chose to put on his product. It meant giving the American manufacturer the power of making repeated advances of duty without requiring Congressional legislation.

---

[35] Hearings, p. 5401.

Miles proceeded to make this clear by a concrete example:

> To illustrate, a certain piece of men's wool suiting, costing
> $1.71 [per yard] in England, costs $2.89 duty paid in New
> York. The price of a duplicate American product is $2.85, not
> because of American costs, but because the tariff permits of
> this high price. Under the proposed American valuation clause
> the duty hereafter would be on the $2.85 price, which would
> bring the imported cloth up to $3.40 when the domestic goods
> might advance to $3.25, which would be the basis for the next
> importation and so on. . . .[36]
>
> In the normal pre-war year 1914 our woolen manufacturers
> had 93.5 per cent of all domestic business, imports being only
> 6.5 per cent. In 1919 they had 99.1 per cent of all domestic
> business. In 1920 they had 97.4 per cent, and imports were
> in the nature of novelties either in design or quality.
>
> When they ask for greater restrictions on imports, higher
> duty, and a Congressional sanction to further raise their prices,
> it is time to question whether this country belongs to the
> people who constitute it or to the manufacturers.[37]

Once more, as he did thirteen years earlier, he admonished the
Congressional law-makers:

> Our nation cannot live in prosperity or honor until Con-
> gress puts every tariff witness under oath, compels him to sub-
> mit his cost books . . . and fixes his rates upon the basis of
> ascertained facts instead of disingenuous conversation. We
> could stand loose ways when competition was in force and
> kept prices down; also when we were not requiring foreign
> markets for our manufacturers. We cannot stand it now, with
> competition weakened or lost, with price-fixing on every hand
> and foreign markets necessary to prosperity.[38]

The significance of these remarks lay in the fact that when they
were first uttered in 1908 it was before the creation of the Tariff
Commission. That he had to repeat his admonition thirteen years
later, with the Tariff Commission in existence but playing no part

[36] Hearings, p. 5381.
[37] Hearings, p. 5382.
[38] Hearings, p. 5416.

in the Congressional tariff enactment, was the saddest aspect of the situation.

Pointing to the two billion dollar "favorable balance" of our foreign trade, measuring the excess of our exports over imports, Miles concluded his testimony with this half retrospective, half prophetic appeal:

> Nothing under Providence will so conduce to our intellectual, cultural and economic developments as this favorable net balance in international trade that other nations can pay only by some $2,000,000,000 of their securities annually accumulated in such fundamental values as water powers, mines, railways, docks, banks, real estate and what not. The wealth of the world is not in money, but in these other things, represented by securities . . . England's world dominance came in this way. She owned a considerable part of the wealth of the United States in our youth and early maturity. Think of England's world-wide understanding, her international ties and appreciations, developed through trade. . . . It is now our turn and in the new brotherhood of nations we will be as safe as is the citizen of one of our states in dealing in another state. Our own breadth of intelligence and our influence will be largely in proportion to our foreign investments.[39]

When the tariff bill reached the Senate floor, the Miles testimony was widely quoted both by Republican and Democratic Senators. But the high protectionists were in control and the Fordney-McCumber Act with the highest rates yet reached in our tariff history was approved by President Harding to become the law of the land.

The protectionists in Congress were aided for the first time in the history of the country by the members from agricultural states which were hard hit by the sudden decline in the prices of grain and cotton from the artificially high war prices. The farmers were told that higher import duties on their products would restore the high prices and they fell for it. Their disappointment in the results that followed and its consequences will be related in the next chapter dealing with the Hawley-Smoot Tariff Act.

[39] Hearings, p. 5419.

VI. THE HAWLEY-SMOOT TARIFF

WHEN HERBERT HOOVER ran for President in 1928, a year of booming prosperity, there was one conspicuously jarring note in the record to which the Republican Party could otherwise "point with pride"—the distress among the farmers.

Abundant crops in the United States and the rest of the world had caused a decline in prices of agricultural products.

The farmers moreover were paying the penalty for having indulged in land speculation during the World War. With Food Administrator Hoover appealing for wheat and more wheat under the slogan "food will win the war;" with a guaranteed price of $2.50 a bushel for all the wheat they could deliver, a speculative fever had developed among the farmers bidding for land. The price of land was driven to dizzy heights, most of it bought subject to mortgage.

When the rest of the world caught up with the demand after the war, while excessive production in the United States kept up, grain prices took a tumble and the farmers were no longer able to keep up payments on the mortgages on land bought at exorbitant prices. Foreclosures followed, many farmers were ruined, and the general economic depression in agriculture was in striking contrast with prosperity in the cities.

Vague promises made by the Republican Party in previous elections had brought no relief and the farmers were in revolt.

It was realized by Republican leaders that something concrete had to be done to hold the farmer vote and in the minds of the Republican politicians the concrete program of relief characteristically took the shape of increased tariff protection on agricultural products.

As an earnest of Republican intentions, Senator Borah exacted a promise from Mr. Hoover in the midst of the Presidential and Congressional campaign that immediately upon his inauguration he would convene a special session of Congress for the purpose of revising the tariff rates on agricultural products.

In fulfillment of that pledge President Hoover convened the Congress in special session on April 15, 1929. In the first sentence of his message to Congress, he said: "I have called this special session of Congress to redeem two pledges given in the last election—farm relief and limited changes in the tariff."

To the credit of Mr. Hoover it should be said that he realized and gave utterance to his conviction that higher tariff rates alone were not going to solve the farmer's problem. In his message he called attention to the "multitude of causes" which brought about the depression in American agriculture and then drew this conclusion:

> Because of the multitude of causes and because agriculture is not one industry, but a score of industries, we are confronted not with a single problem alone but a great number of problems. Therefore there is no single plan or principle that can be generally applied. Some of the forces working to the detriment of agriculture can be greatly mitigated by improving our waterway transportation; some of them by readjustment of the tariff; some by better understanding and adjustment of production needs; and some by improvement in the methods of marketing.

Hoover spoke as an engineer and economist, seeking constructive long-range methods to bring down the cost of production of agricultural products. He spoke over the heads of the politicians in Congress who preferred the direct method of securing immediate results without regard to the soundness of the method as a permanent solution of the problem. The Republican politicians saw such a remedy in a higher tariff, while, later, the Democratic politicians under the succeeding Roosevelt administration found it in parity-price laws artificially raising prices of farm products by government fiat. Neither set of politicians had the wisdom nor the patience for fundamental long-term measures which their respective leaders, Hoover, and Wilson, envisaged.

No sooner did the Ways and Means Committee get down to work on tariff revision than it became apparent that in utter disregard of the pre-election pledge of a "limited" revision of the tariff, to which President Hoover referred in his message, it was set to revise the entire tariff with the object of raising the Fordney-McCumber rates of 1922, at that time the highest in the history of the country, to new dizzy heights. In vain did Borah and other Senators representing agricultural states protest. In vain did they point to the fact that there had been no demand for higher duties on manufactured goods during the election campaign, that the farmer had suffered in the past from selling his products in an unprotected market and buying everything he needed from plows to clothing, in a highly protected market; that the object of a limited revision of the tariff was to compensate the farmer for the handicaps he had suffered as a buyer with new advantages that increased duties on his products would give him as a seller. If increased duties on farm products were to be accompanied by still higher duties on manufactured products, the farmer would be left where he was before tariff revision. Their pleas fell on deaf ears.

Once more Miles girded his loins for a fight against the new tariff raid, as he had done on previous occasions over a period of nearly a quarter of a century. This time Miles made his contribution in the form of studies of various aspects of the tariff in his capacity of President of the Fair Tariff League. The studies were made with the aid of experts and were passed on to various Senators who spread them on the pages of the Congressional Record. Among

[101]

these Senators, belonging to the Progressive wings of both the Republican and Democratic Parties, were Brookhart, Harrison, Norbeck, Norris, Nye, Walsh, Wheeler.

As the Congress had been convened for the express purpose of raising the tariff on farm products, Miles addressed himself to the task of demonstrating how ineffectual the tariff was when applied to agriculture. With the aid of economists in the Bureau of Agricultural Economics and the Bureau of the Census he prepared elaborate estimates contrasting the "nominal," i.e., the legal duty levied under the law and the "effective" protection as measured by the difference between the price of, say, wheat in Liverpool and Chicago.

Five of these studies were discussed and spread on the pages of the Congressional Record by Senator Brookhart, Republican of Iowa on June 18 (pp. 3024–29) and November 12, 1929 (pp. 5439–54).

The results of the study were summed up in an elaborate table containing nearly all the farm products subject to duty under the Fordney and Hawley-Smoot tariffs.

These products were presented in two groups: Group 1 including wheat, corn, oats, barley, rye, rice, flaxseed, potatoes, onions, lemons, figs, peanuts, walnuts, almonds, hay, tobacco, hogs and eggs showed a striking divergence between the nominal, i.e., legal protection and the effective protection as measured by the excess of the domestic prices over the world price. The nominal duty for the group as a whole was found to be 36.2% ad valorem as against only 1.1% effective duty under the Fordney-McCumber tariff and 46% as against 1.3% under the Hawley-Smoot bill.

In other words, raising the tariff from 36% under the Fordney tariff to 46% under the Hawley-Smoot bill was going to benefit the farmer only two-tenths of one per cent—from 1.1% to 1.3%.

In contrast to this was Group 2 including butter, cattle, wool and sugar. Unlike the products in group 1, which were largely produced in abundance in the United States and yielded a surplus for export, those in group 2 had to be imported to supplement domestic production in order to meet domestic demand. For these products the nominal tariff was fully effective. Thus the nominal duty on wool was 52% under the Fordney Act and was fully effective, i.e., it made the domestic price 52% higher than the world price. The same was true of sugar.

In the case of butter and cattle, while the duty was more effective than for products in group 1, it was not 100% effective since the domestic demand did not have to be satisfied wholly by imports, the bulk coming from domestic production. Thus the nominal (i.e., legal) duty on butter under the Fordney Act was 251.6% ad valorem, while its effective rate was 105%, meaning that the domestic price of butter was 105% above the price in Canada. The proposed increase of the duty to 293.6% under the Hawley-Smoot tariff would still leave the effective rate at 105%. Similarly the nominal duty of 250% on cattle under the Fordney Act produced an effective rate of 45%. Its increase to 333% under the Hawley-Smoot bill would still leave the effective rate at 45%.

In contrast with the ineffectiveness of the tariff on farm products produced in the United States in abundance, Miles drew a picture of the perniciously effective way the tariff on manufactured products was made to serve as a concealed tax on the consumer—a tax imposed by trusts or combinations of manufacturers controlling the market for their respective products.

On November 11, 1929 Senator Norris spread on the Congressional Record an elaborate table submitted by Miles, showing the effect of the tariff on steel and metal products. This was further elaborated in a statement published in the record on January 23, 1930, again by Senator Norris.

In both statements Miles hammered away at the tariff as a concealed tax levied by manufacturers on consumers.

Pointing out that high duties resulted in dwindling imports from which the Government derived a relatively small revenue, he proceeded to estimate the extra revenue private manufacturers derived or could derive by adding the amount of the tariff to the competitive price they would otherwise have to charge. Dividing the steel industry into two groups, the first comprising seven heavy steel products of pig iron, bar steel, steel rails, tin plate, structural iron and steel, cast and wrought iron pipe and wire and wire products, and the second, consisting of highly finished products from cutlery to locomotives and machine tools, he compared the revenue the Government derived from the tariff on the imports of these products with the domestic production, and came to the following conclusion:

For each dollar of tariff revenue the Government collected on the imports of the following products,

```
Hardware manufacturers allowed in extra profits of _____$ 1,726
Bolts and nuts manufacturers allowed in extra profits of ____  1,617
Cutlery manufacturers allowed in extra profits of _____     23
Electrical machinery manufacturers allowed in extra profits of  1,340
Screws, for wood manufacturers allowed in extra profits of __  1,340
Cash registers manufacturers allowed in extra profits of ____  3,879
Stamped and enameled ware manufacturers allowed in extra
  profits of _____    449
Tinware manufacturers allowed in extra profits of _____ 20,385
```

It should be said parenthetically that while in the case of several products subject to monopoly control, the price in the United States was higher than in foreign countries by approximately the amount of the tariff, it was not invariably true of products in which domestic competition prevailed to a greater or less degree, especially when supply exceeded demand. Miles lacked the means and facilities for an elaborate and costly study to trace the exact extent to which various industries took advantage of the tariff. In many cases

Miles' figures reflected the actual state of affairs. In others they showed the potential mischief which the tariff rates represented.

While Miles was submitting his estimates, another public spirited manufacturer, W. T. Rawleigh, from the neighboring state of Illinois, who owed a large part of his wealth to the protection his spices and condiments enjoyed under the tariff, undertook two special studies to answer that very question of the effect of the tariff on domestic prices. His only connection with the studies was to finance them, leaving the actual work of ascertaining the facts and drawing conclusions to the men he entrusted with the studies.

The first of these studies, covering agricultural products, was carried on by a staff headed by Prof. Walter A. Morton under the supervision of three well-known economists on the faculty of the University of Wisconsin—John R. Commons, Selig Perlman and Benjamin H. Hibbard.

The other study dealing with manufactured products was in charge of David J. Lewis, a lawyer who had had considerable experience in that field as a former member of the Tariff Commission.

These reports were made available to Congress by Mr. Rawleigh and were likewise published in the Congressional Record of January 11, 1930 (pp. 1436–1461) on the initiative of Senator Robert M. La Follette, Jr.

The study of manufactured products could not include all the tens of thousands of articles covered by the tariff. In the introduction to his report Mr. Lewis stated:

> The list of articles studied is by no means comprehensive. That would be impossible because the tariff bill covers in its specific paragraphs about 10,000 commodities and in its "basket clauses" hundreds of thousands more. They are, however, typical of the kind and character of increases proposed in the bill and omit entirely some of the larger and more indefensible raises in rates.

The study covered a wide range of commodities in common use such as earthen ware, china, bricks, cement, various kinds of glass, glassware and hand blown glass bottles; pig iron, cast iron pipe, watches, razor blades, surgical and scientific instruments, wooden shingles, furniture, ropes and cordage, woolen carpets and rugs, men's and boy's clothing, other wearing apparel, rayon and rayon goods, toys and dolls, agate buttons, leather boots and shoes.

The study compared existing prices (in 1929) under the Fordney tariff with prewar prices in 1913. It found that in all cases of manufactured goods subject to market price control through combinations among producers, the tariff was added to the price.

In addition to high prices swelled by the tariff, the study reported excessive profits made by the manufacturers of these commodities, of which one example may be mentioned. The Lehigh Portland Cement Company, in addition to paying dividends continuously since 1899 from 3 to 7%, paid a stock dividend of 128% in 1900; the next year another stock dividend of 58% followed, "and at various intervals since further dividends ranging from 20 to 100%, the last being in 1928 when was created a 7% preferred cumulative stock issue of $22,517,400 in shares having a par value of $100 each." This resulted in an increase of an original investment of $100 to $3,420 in common stock and $3,420 in 7% cumulative preferred, making the dividends on the original investment of $100 equal to $470.80 or 479% in 1929, the year the Hawley-Smoot Act was under consideration in Congress. All this happened with cement duty free. Yet the Hawley-Smoot bill chose to "protect" the industry by a duty of 8 cents per 100 lbs.

Similar fantastic profits were cited in other industries covered by the study.

The study by the Wisconsin University economists of the effect of the tariff on farm products reached the same conclusion as that by the Government economists who contributed to the Miles study, viz., that the tariff had no effect on prices of most of the farm products which are produced in the United States in abundance leaving a surplus for export, while in the case of products such as clothing—wool and sugar whose domestic production is so small that the domestic demand must be satisfied largely by imports from other countries, the tariff is effective, i.e., it is added to the world price of these commodities.

Another aspect of the tariff which Miles undertook to clarify at this time was the varying effect of the tariff on different States of the Union. In a series of studies Miles proceeded to show how some industrial states in the East were enabled by the tariff to take advantage of agricultural states in the West and South. These studies bore such titles as: What New Jersey Gets Out of the Tariff (Congressional Record, November 11, 1929), What Massachusetts Gets Out of the Tariff (Congressional Record, November 7, 1929), What the Tariff Does to Iowa (Congressional Record, November 12, 1929), etc. He summed these up in a study spread on the pages of the Congressional Record of November 12, 1929 (p. 5441) by Senator Brookhart in which Miles contrasted the profits which a few leading manufacturing states in the East enjoyed as against the losses sustained by a few typical agricultural states in the West and South in the following table:

PROFITS

New Jersey	$ 813,000,000
Pennsylvania	1,393,000,000
Massachusetts	814,000,000
Connecticut	386,000,000
Rhode Island	207,000,000
New York	1,800,000,000

LOSSES

Western States

Nebraska	$ 66,000,000
Wisconsin	129,000,000
South Dakota	31,000,000
Washington	77,000,000
Idaho	22,000,000
Colorado	47,000,000
Minnesota	123,000,000
Kansas	86,000,000

Southern States

Texas	197,000,000
Georgia	109,000,000
Florida	41,818,000

The profits of the Eastern States were estimated on the basis of the production of their important industries. The estimates of losses of the agricultural states were based on the estimated overpayments by the consumers of those states based on their respective populations, and deducting from these losses what they gained on their protected products such as wood, wheat, sugar beets, dairy products, etc.

Without attempting to pass upon the accuracy or completeness of these estimates, it is obvious that they served to present a true picture of contrasts between the industrial states which were net gainers under the tariff as against the agricultural states which were net losers.

The picture has since been radically changed not through the tariff on agricultural products, but through the device of artificially raising the prices of agricultural products through Government support under the so-called parity price laws.

In discussing the Hawley-Smoot tariff Bill in the Senate on November 12, 1929, Senator Brookhart remarked:

Of the eleven Republican members of the Senate Finance Committee who wrote the Senate bill, 5 are from New England, Pennsylvania and New Jersey. Two are western wool and sugar men, with like predatory desires. This has been the general character of this committee for a generation.

It is not clear who wrote the tariff and to what purpose.

There was not a nationally minded representative of consumers or farmers among them. None wanted, of course.

The Senate bill is tainted with self-interest. It offers no basis for action.

Congress is stalled.

Under the circumstances, it is not surprising that Miles' contribution to the consideration of the Hawley-Smoot tariff failed to produce results, the kind of results that he and Rawleigh, two knights errant of the industrial empire sought to produce: putting an end to extortion from the common people made legal by the tariff. As so often happens, the unorganized consumer fell easy prey to organized greed. The Hawley-Smoot bill in spite of its complete reversal of the policy outlined in the President's message in fulfillment of pre-election pledges, was approved by President Hoover and became the law of the land and is still in force as this story is published in 1952. Many of its rates of duty, however, have been successively reduced under the reciprocity treaties initiated by Secretary of State, Cordell Hull in 1934 and repeatedly renewed under special acts of Congress.

VII. MILES ON TRUSTS

IF THERE was one outstanding conclusion that Miles drew from his life-long study of the tariff, it was that the tariff was a breeder of trusts and that the trusts, by which he meant any successful organization or combination to control prices, used the tariff as an effective tool for controlling and raising prices.

This naturally led him to a study of trusts, a subject which, with the tariff, absorbed his interest.

The organization of Code Authorities under the NRA (National Recovery Administration) stirred him to violent opposition. Each code authority obtained complete control over prices in its industry. This, notwithstanding the provision in the Recovery Act "that such codes shall not permit monopolies or monopolistic practices."

Before the Supreme Court had rendered its famous unanimous decision which outlawed the National Recovery Act, Miles appeared on April 18, 1935 before the Senate Committee on Finance with a statement in which he presented a scathing indictment of the Department of Justice which he charged with deliberate failure to prosecute the trusts and combinations effectively under the Sherman Anti-Trust Act. He charged the two Roosevelts with shadow boxing with the trusts, while letting them get away with public plunder.

He paid his respects to the wisdom and honesty of the Supreme Court which he called "the bulwark of our liberties." However, said Miles,

. . . the Supreme Court is as dead and useless as a parked automobile unless and until an outside force steps on the gas and releases its energies. The Attorney-General is the outside force. He is under oath to act. . . .

[110]

My study with the assistance and advice of able counsel assures me that, as my advisers say, the Attorneys-General have, without important exceptions, and for 30 years, as respects monopoly, made of the Supreme Court "a lion in a showman's cage with the Attorney-General holding the key."

Miles proceeded to cite important trust cases brought before the Supreme Court with important evidence of price fixing lacking, though amply available. He regarded the National Recovery Act with its industrial codes as the legalization of the trusts though in flagrant violation of the anti-trust laws. His view was validated within a month by the Supreme Court decision outlawing the National Recovery Act.

VIII. CONCLUSION

MILES, THE hard-headed business man, the gadfly of special interests, and scourge of dishonest politicians, was in his private life a radiant spirit with an extraordinary capacity for compassing other lives in his genial warmth and for rejoicing in other people's progress and achievements.

He showed this toward his brother who on graduating from college entered the business they both looked forward to working in together. When the brother's thoughts turned toward the ministry, both felt uncertain whether his place was in business where all family traditions pointed, or in the new field to which he was drawn. True to his sympathy for new ventures, Miles finally said: "If this business succeeds, one of us is enough to be in it, and if it does not, one is surely enough." A few years later, writing to his brother on the day he entered on his first pastorate, he said:

> "This is a queer world and as I get older it seems the stranger. I started out so very desirous of doing some great good to men and thought I could through business. I am just now wondering whether I can do or not. I must soon, or I never can."

All through life he endeavored to do some significant good to men, first in his relations with his employees, his customers, and later, as we have seen, in his life-long fight for honesty and the public good in national and state legislation. The wasting and wrecking of young lives among the underprivileged stirred him to his depths.

He was instrumental in having his native state, Wisconsin, adopt the system of continuation schools with vocational guidance, thus setting an example for other states to follow. He was the first President of the Wisconsin State Board for Vocational Education, holding that office for six years until he resigned in 1917 to take charge of the division in the Council of National Defense responsible for training war workers in munition plants throughout the country. Vocational schools, their establishment and development in Wisconsin, claimed his attention for the rest of his life, as tariff reform and the fight against monopoly absorbed his energies in his activities on the national scene.

Writing to his brother in December 1899 when he was 39 years old, he said: "I am tired of making money." It was soon after, that he first became painfully aware of the effect of the tariff on his own business and small business generally, and plunged into the fight which eventually resulted in the establishment of the Tariff Board in 1909.

As time went on, it became increasingly difficult to keep up the fight on behalf of the public and stay in business; not only because of the burden of doing both, but because he found that his business responsibilities cramped him in his public activities:

> I have remarkable data (he wrote to his brother in February 1912). I want to use it. But interested friends, all unpatriotic in trying to prevent me, and some very sweet and able friends also say no, 'twill hurt me dreadfully and do no good. I know it will almost damn me and make me classed with ranters and hare-brains, but I do want to go to it and help stop the awful condition. It saps our public and private life.

Soon after writing this letter he quit business in his fifty-third year. He took a much needed rest enjoying for a time the care-free life of California, but he could not long remain idle and he could not give up his public work. The tariff and vocational training absorbed most of his energies and time for the remaining twenty six years of his life.

His fight for an "honest tariff", carried on over a period of more than thirty years, failed in its immediate objective. The Hawley-Smoot Act raised the rates far beyond the Payne-Aldrich Act which he had denounced more than twenty years before. The principle of determining a fair measure of protection by the difference in costs at home and abroad was lost sight of in the Hawley-Smoot Act. The Tariff Commission, from which he had expected so much, was debauched by the Harding and Coolidge appointments and had a negligible, if any, part in the enactment of the Fordney and Hawley-Smoot Tariffs. All this could not but affect a man of Miles' sensitiveness. Writing to me late in November, 1938, less than a year before his death, he said:

> You know I was an optimist, believing that a beneficent God guided us, and that even I, as everyone, by hard work and good, made for goodness.
>
> But for years recently I've seen no good in mankind fundamentally. If good things come to him he seems good. Otherwise he shames the beasts.

But giving way to pessimism was not in the nature of Herbert Miles, not even in his seventy-ninth year. Six months later, under date of May 27, 1939 he wrote to me concerning the book on which he had been at work for some time. His letter shows his unsuccessful fight for the tariff had served only to broaden his vision:

> The book as respects conclusions is everything except tariff. Tariff may be the particular cause and means, but the things to mend are the price structure, monopoly, fundamental honesty, and six to ten other definite great subjects among which may well be public education. Also, in particular, a redefinition of the capitalistic system.
>
> 'Til just now that system has meant to me that each person must create wealth or get it by will of a creator and that that wealth is his for all good reasons, and the great incentive.

Just now, I think I see that half the people see in capitalism the stolen possession of wealth created by others. I hate that as much as Communists do.

On this basis, there are two kinds of capitalism, that of Ford, Carnegie, Chrysler, and a million men who earn, create. Then there is what is now the more overwhelming capitalism that represents only stolen goods and is indicated by the twenty-five billion dollars that Pecora says was gotten by the New York stock exchange people through the sale, in recent years of worthless securities. A society ruled by such people is cursed. One dominated by the Ford wealth-creating kind is blessed. I think the distinction worth stating with provisions for the conserving of the wealth-creating capitalism and the destruction of the other—all after the fashion of the Commandments.

A little over two months after writing that letter, on August 6, 1939, Herbert Miles died.

Although he failed in his effort to get reasonable rates under the Hawley-Smoot Act, he had the satisfaction of seeing their substantial reduction through the Hull Reciprocity Agreements. While the Republican majority in the Eightieth Congress was able in 1948 to restrict the powers of the Executive to grant concessions under reciprocity agreements, which have been further curtailed by the Republican-Dixie Democratic coalition in the eighty-first and eighty-second Congresses, the system of reciprocity agreements still prevails. What the future holds in store would be hazardous to predict, but certain trends can be noted.

Miles' failure, like McKinley's before him, was due in part to the backwardness and immaturity of political thought of the American voter, caused to a considerable extent by the physical isolation of the country between two oceans. A century ago England, having emerged from the Napoleonic wars as the strongest and most advanced industrial country and greatest creditor nation in the world, realized that she must let her debtor nations pay their obligations to her in goods, not gold. Richard Cobden and John Bright aroused the nation to its new role and by striking off the shackles of protection England rose to world leadership which remained unchallenged for nearly a century until the two World Wars exhausted her accumulated wealth and she became a debtor nation.

The United States has now emerged from the two World Wars as the undisputed world leader, yet seems unable to shed the swaddling clothes of the tariff which originally was intended for the protection of infant industries.

Half a century after McKinley's clarion call for reciprocity, when he announced that "the time of exclusiveness is past", sectional and local interests are still able to defeat the efforts of those who are concerned with the larger interests of the nation.

The alignment of interests with regard to the tariff has undergone a radical change since the turn of the century. In the past, the lines were clearly drawn: manufacturers in the East and North for protection, the farmers in the West and South generally against. Since the adoption of the Hawley-Smoot tariff the farmers have been largely won over to protection. The South, too, with its growing industries has become strongly protectionist, while a large and growing and most important section of industry in the East and North which formerly constituted the backbone of protection is raising its sights toward foreign fields. The two leading national organizations which speak for business with authority—the Chamber of Commerce of the United States and the National Association of Manufacturers—reflect Miles' viewpoint in favoring the extension of reciprocity through mutual tariff reductions.

Their spokesmen, men of the type of Paul G. Hoffman who won his spurs in the heat of the competitive struggle and is an acknowledged leader in the advanced thinking of big business, are conscious of the industrial might and superiority of America and are not afraid of foreign competition. They see in foreign trade an indispensable outlet for the surplus output of our gigantic industrial set-up. They realize that the only way other nations can pay for our huge exports is by selling us goods which they can produce more cheaply or better than we can and that the resulting increased two-way trade is bound to benefit both sides.

It is this new alignment and thinking of business interests, rather than a possible revolt of the unorganized consumers, that holds out the promise of freer, if not free, trade.

The seed planted by Miles, trampled under ground by hostile forces, may yet sprout and see the light of day as our world interests continue to expand.

INDEX

Page

Agar, James S. ----------------- 59
Agricultural Products --------99–103
Aldrich, Senator --------39, 62–64, 66
Allison Tariff Commission ------64, 65
American Reciprocal Tariff League-7, 59

Batchelder, Nahum I ------------ 59
Beveridge, Albert, Senator
----------------31, 39, 40, 60, 67
Bright, John -------------------- 116
Brookhart, Senator ------102, 107, 108
Burgess, Wm. -----------------69, 72
Butler, Nicholas Murray -------- 60

Cannon, Joseph, Speaker ----33, 34, 66
Carnegie, Andrew -------------- 51
Cement profits under tariff ------ 106
Cobden, Richard --------------- 116
Committee of 100 for a Tariff
Commission --------------- 60
Commons, John R., Prof. ------- 105
Coolidge, Calvin, President ------ 76
Costigan, Edward P. ----------69, 76
Cuba, sugar and the tariff ------85–88
pineapples and the tariff--89–92
Culbertson, Wm. S. -----------68, 76
Cummings, Congressman -------- 77
Senator ------------- 67
Customs revenue -------------- 23

Dalzell, Congressman ---------54, 55
Depression agricultural -------99, 100
Dingley Tariff Act ---5, 6, 9, 39, 44, 45

Emery, Henry C. ---------------- 68
Export trade hampered by tariff--11–15

Fair Tariff League
----------69, 77, 82, 89, 93, 101
Farmer attitude on tariff -------- 98
Farm products, tariff--99–103, 105–109

Page

Finance Committee, Senate---8, 82, 108
Ford ------------------------- 115
Fordney, Congressman ---------- 54
Fordney–McCumber Tariff Act
------------85, 93–98, 102, 106

German Tariff ----------------- 7, 9
Glassie, Henry H. -------------69–76
Guild, Curtis ------------------ 59

Harding, Warren G. President---- 69
Harrison, Senator -------------- 102
Harvey, George ---------------- 32
Hawley–Smoot Tariff ------85, 99–109
Hibbard, Benjamin H. ---------- 105
Hides, Tariff on ---------------11, 12
Hoffman, Paul ----------------- 116
Home Market Club ------------ 76
Hoover, Herbert, President
------------------87, 99–101, 109
Hosiery, tariff, prices ----------94, 95
Howard, Wm. ----------------- 68
Hull, Cordell ----------------- 109

Iron, pig --------------------- 13

Johnstone, Alva --------------- 59

Kasson, John A.
Kasson Reciprocity Treaties ---- 6
Kent, Wm. -------------------- 69
Kirby, John

La Follette, Robert M. Senator
-------------------31, 39, 40, 62
La Follette, R. M. Jr. Senator ---- 105
Leather, tariff ----------------11, 12
Lewis, David J. --69, 74, 76, 105, 106
Lodge, Henry Cabot, Senator ---- 67
Longworth, Nicholas, Congr. ---- 67
Lumber, Tariff ---------------- 15

Page

Manufacturers, Nat'l Association
  --------------4, 8, 10, 16, 21, 39
Marvin, Thomas O. ----69–71, 72, 75
McKinley Wm., President ----5, 6, 116
Miles, Herbert E.
  Birth, death ----------------- 3
  Report to Nat'l Ass'n of Agr'l
    Impl. & Vehicle Mnf. -----11–20
  Report to Nat'l Ass'n of Mnfrs.
    -----------------------21–29, 39
  Pamphlet: The Old Way and the
    New Way ----------------34–37
  Demand for a Tariff Com'n ---- 38
  Nat'l Tariff Com'n Conv'n ---- 60
  Attack on Special Interests on
    Tariff Commission --------70–76
  Congr'l Committees -------76–78
  Attack on Sugar Tariff ------82–88
  on Fordney–McCumber Tariff--93–98
  New definition of protection
    ----------------------32, 79–81
  tariff and effective protection--102–104
  tariff on pineapples ---------89–92
  vocational guidance --------112–113
Monopoly (see also Trusts) ----- 42
Morton, Walter A. Prof. -------- 105
Nat'l Ass'n Agr. Impl. & Vehic.
  Mnfr. -----------------8, 10–21
Nat'l Ass'n of Mnfrers--8, 21–30, 39, 62
NRA (nat'l Recov. Admin.) ----- 110
Norbeck, Senator -------------- 102
Norris, Senator -------------102, 103
Nye, Senator ----------------- 102
Page, Thomas W. -------------- 68
Parry, D. M. ----------------59, 60
Payne, Sereno ----33–36, 49, 56, 62, 66
Perlman, Selig, Prof. ----------- 105
Pig iron, cost of prod. tariff ----- 13
Pineapples, production, tariff ---89–92
Prices and tariff ----15, 16, 53, 78, 106
    export ------------------- 15
    domestic ----------------- 15
Profits and tariff -------------80, 106
Protect. tariff definition
  ----------------32, 70, 79–81, 89
Rawleigh, W. T. ---------------- 105

Page

Reciprocity
  Kasson treaties -------------- 6
  Movement ------6–11, 17, 27, 40, 59
Republican platform ------------ 45
Reynolds, Jas. B. -------------- 68
Roosevelt, Theodore, Pres.--7, 34, 38, 60

Sanders, Alvin H. --------7–10, 59, 68
Senate Finance Committee ---8, 82, 108
Smoot, Senator
  Hawley–Smoot Tariff ----86, 99–109
Standard Oil ------------------- 5
Steel, Tariff ----4, 5, 13–15, 51, 52, 104
  export price -------------- 14
  domestic price ----------- 14
Sugar tariff ------------70, 77, 79–88
Supreme Court -------------110–111

Taft, William H. President---8, 30, 38,
      44–46, 50, 60, 62, 63, 66–68
Tariff ------------------------ 10
  ad valorem basis ------------96–97
  agricultural products -------99–103
  Board ---------------------- 66
  cement --------------------- 106
  Commission --- 67, 68, 69, 89, 91–92
  Commission movement--9, 25, 26, 30–
      34, 38–39, 59–64, 67
  Dingley Act ---------------- 5, 6
  dual ----------------------- 6
  Fair Tariff League ------69–70, 77,
      82, 89, 93, 101
  farm products -----99–103, 105, 107
  Fordney–McCumber -----93–98, 106
  German --------------------- 7–8
  hides ---------------------11–12
  hosiery --------------------94–95
  lobbyists ------------------69, 72
  leather --------------------11–12
  lumber --------------------- 15
  McKinley ------------------- 5, 6
  and Monopoly -----------42, 51, 53
  oil, mineral ---------------- 52
  pig iron -------------------- 13
  and prices
    4, 12, 14, 15, 39, 95, 97, 104–107

	Page
protection, definition and measure of	79–81
reciprocity	6–8, 17
Republican platform	45
for revenue	23
steel	14
sugar	79–88
Wilson Act	5, 48
Taussig, Frank W. Prof.	68
Tompkins, D. A.	59

	Page
Towne, Henry R.	59
Trusts	5, 42, 51, 110–111
U. S. Steel Corp.	5
Van Cleve, James	33, 44, 50, 59, 60, 62
Walsh, Senator	102
Wheeler, Senator	102
Wilson, Woodrow, President	67, 68
Wilson Tariff Act	5, 48
Wisconsin University tariff study	105–108